A Perennial Faith

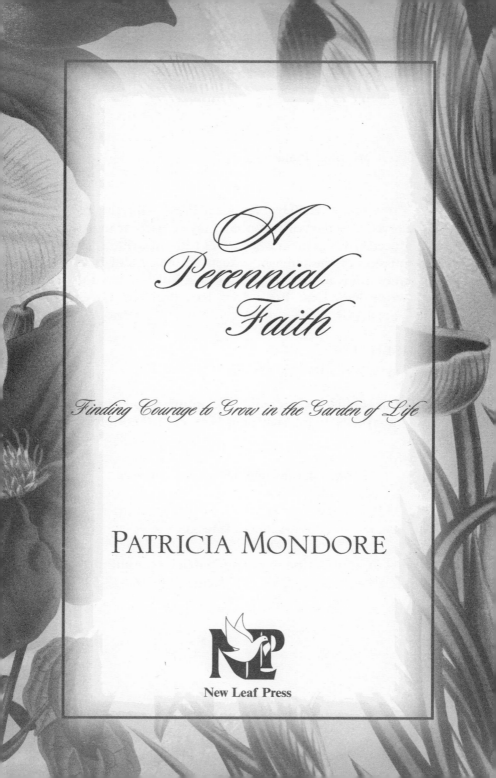

A Perennial Faith

Finding Courage to Grow in the Garden of Life

PATRICIA MONDORE

New Leaf Press

First printing: January 2001

ISBN: 0-89221-504-6
Library of Congress Number: 00-110217

Unless otherwise noted, all Scripture references are from the New International Version of the Bible.

Printed in the United States of America.

Please visit our website for other great titles:
www.newleafpress.net

For information regarding publicity for author interviews contact Dianna Fletcher at (870) 438-5288.

Contents

It wasn't all that long ago when I was known as the person who couldn't even keep silk flowers alive. What is the opposite of a green thumb? Orange, perhaps? That was me. Whether it was a houseplant or a tulip bulb in the garden, I was convinced I was an utter failure when it came to gardening. All that changed abruptly, however, when we moved into our own home. The property came with a large but completely unlandscaped backyard which suddenly appeared to me as a clean palette waiting to be decorated. So I went out and cautiously began experimenting. First it was a pack of sunflower seeds, then a little evergreen tree, and before long I was hooked. This former orange thumb is now absolutely enthralled with gardening and it has become a year-round pastime (I try to avoid the word "obsession"). I spend my winters reading the magazines and laying out new plans. On the first day of spring I'm out digging and planting, then watering and weeding all summer, followed by picking and cleaning up in the fall.

I had always heard that gardening was relaxing. People told me it would take my mind off of work and be a nice hobby or diversion. I found out that it is, indeed, all of those things, but it is also something much more. What no one ever told me was that as I spent time in the garden I would find myself drawn closer to the Master Gardener himself. As I work with the earth, plant my seeds, watch new life spring forth and burst forth into glorious blooms of color, I can't help but see the hands of God at work. In fact, in every minute detail I have discovered little inspirational messages that have delighted my heart, lifted my spirit, and deepened my faith. My prayer, as I share some of these little gleanings from my garden, is that they will do the same for you. Come join me now as we head out to the backyard together.

God's Garden

Now the LORD God had planted a garden in the east, in Eden; and there he put the man he had formed (Gen. 2:8).

Actually, it makes perfect sense that one would feel close to God in a garden. The very first place God put man and woman after He made them was in the garden He had personally prepared for them. The One who formed the entire universe chose a little plot of soil on one small planet and planted a garden, and He did it all for us. It was, of course, practical to start mankind out in a garden since it could provide an immediate source of food for us newcomers. However, God had much more than food in mind. We read, "And the LORD God made all kinds of trees grow out of the ground — trees that were pleasing to the eye and good for food. In the middle of the garden were the tree of life and the tree of the knowledge of good and evil" (Gen. 2:9). This lovely garden in paradise was designed with all three of the needs unique to mankind in mind.

Unlike anything else He created, only we

humans were physical, emotional, and spiritual beings. The garden would sustain us physically by providing the nutrition our bodies needed to function. It also fed our souls by giving us purpose and pleasure. We are told, "The LORD God took the man and put him in the Garden of Eden to work it and take care of it" (Gen. 2:15). God certainly didn't need caretakers, but He knew that giving us this responsibility would allow mankind to be both productive and creative which is essential to our emotional well-being. But He also made us with a spiritual need that He alone could fill. He knew that there in the garden we could meet the Master Gardener himself. Each plant, tree, and flower draws us closer to the One who formed it since, as He intended, all of creation reveals its maker to us. Because He made everything in it, every garden is God's garden. It is no wonder one can feel His presence there.

Then the man and his wife heard the sound of the LORD God as he was walking in the garden in the cool of the day, and they hid from the LORD God among the trees of the garden (Gen. 3:8).

It was in a garden that God, himself, first came and visited mankind. He created Adam and Eve and then He came and walked with them there in the gardens He had custom made for them. He must have enjoyed seeing those He had made in His own image prospering in the lovely idyllic setting so lovingly prepared for them. Every need they had — body, soul, and spirit — was abundantly provided there. At least that's how it was in the beginning. The Garden was also the place where mankind failed the first spiritual test, that of simple trust and obedience. Despite God's warnings and the fact that every one of her needs had already been met, Eve allowed herself to be tricked into eating from the one tree that was off limits to her. Had she only rejected the tempter's lure, she could have lived forever in paradise with her Creator.

But let's not be too hard on Eve. We have

continued in her footsteps when it comes to faith and obedience to God. While we point the fingers at her for eating the forbidden fruit, we are no less guilty when we knowingly make wrong or selfish choices. We are all to blame that our world today is filled with hatred, poverty, pollution, and war. There is good news, however, and it was first discovered in the Garden. There, Adam and Eve found grace. Even though they failed Him, God remained faithful to mankind. They could no longer live in Eden because of their wrong choices, but God never stopped loving Adam and Eve. In fact, He blessed them with over 900 years of life and they learned to plant gardens of their own. Yes, true to His word and faithful to His promises, God provided for Adam and Eve, and through them came all the rest of mankind including Jesus. And He came to bring eternal life back to mankind. Our story ends in salvation, but it all began in a garden.

Cursed is the ground because of you; through painful toil you will eat of it all the days of your life. It will produce thorns and thistles for you, and you will eat the plants of the field (Gen. 3:17–18).

What's the difference between wildflowers and garden flowers? Actually, not much. In fact, botanists tell us that every garden flower we have today originally was a wildflower. By careful selection and cross-pollination of the finest plants, wildflowers were used to produce every modern species of garden flower. Today's garden flowers, however, bear little resemblance to their wild ancestors. Plant breeders have improved flowers by two main methods: hybridization and crossbreeding. Their goal is to combine in one individual plant the desirable characteristics found in different plants. After several generations of carefully selecting only the most perfect specimens, the desired effect is usually achieved. Larger blossoms, new colors, longer blooming periods, hardiness, and disease resistance are but a few of the traits that can be developed by hybridizing.

All the garden flowers of today were brought

about by careful crossbreeding of wildflowers. But one might be tempted to ask where, then, did the wildflowers come from? If we go all the way back to the beginning we find that wildflowers could only have come from garden flowers. Before there was any mention of weeds or wildflowers, the Bible first described the lush and beautiful Garden of Eden. There, we read, "The land produced vegetation: plants bearing seed according to their kinds and trees bearing fruit with seed in it according to their kinds. And God saw that it was good" (Gen. 1:12). It all began there, but once sin entered the world even the plant life felt the effects. Only then did the land begin to produce thorns and thistles and, most likely, wildflowers. Thankfully, one of God's gifts to mankind was to give us the ability to till the land, to plant gardens and, in a small way, to recreate the garden-like setting that existed prior to the Fall. Today, as we enjoy our stunningly beautiful hybridized flowers, we have been granted but a taste of good things to come that will be even better than "in the beginning."

"I have set my rainbow in the clouds, and it will be the sign of the covenant between me and the earth" (Gen. 9:13).

One of the most colorful gardening catalogs I ever saw contained only one flower. But that one flower comes in over 200 species that cover every color of the rainbow. In fact, this flower came to be called the iris precisely because of all those colors. The iris takes its name from Greek for rainbow because of its many different colors. Iris, in Greek mythology, was the goddess of the rainbow. She was represented as a lovely maiden with wings and robes of bright colors, and a halo of light on her head trailing across the sky with a rainbow in her wake. She was also the messenger between the gods and mankind. As the myth goes, she would only leave Olympus to convey the divine commands of Zeus and his wife to humans. So when one saw the rainbow in the sky it was Iris bearing some kind of message from the gods.

Now as colorful as that story is, the real story far outdoes any myth. The rainbow is not some mythological messenger but it is a message sent directly from the God of the universe to mankind. A flood had nearly destroyed the earth but because of His great love for us God gave mankind another chance. The message of the rainbow was that He promised to never again allow such a flood to destroy the earth. The capricious gods of Greek mythology were continually changing their minds and their messages. The God of the Bible is an unchanging, ever-loving God and His rainbow brought the message of a covenant He made between himself and mankind. He declared, "Whenever the rainbow appears in the clouds, I will see it and remember the everlasting covenant between God and all living creatures of every kind on the earth" (Gen. 9:16). So, next time you see an iris in bloom think of the message its rainbow colors bears. It is the message of love and hope from the One who never breaks His promises.

Pure White

You are to be holy to me because I, the LORD, am holy, and I have set you apart from the nations to be my own (Lev. 20:26).

My mother-in-law told me she got her first peony as a housewarming gift back in the 1950s and every summer thereafter was greeted with a dazzling display of pure white flowers. She enjoyed them so much that after a few years she decided to plant a second peony just across the yard from the first. The new plant was bright pink and the first year it flowered, the contrast between the snowy white and the brilliant pink blooms was stunning. As the years went by, however, a rather surprising change began to take place in the white peony. At first, it was just a few tiny speckles of pink appearing in some of the white petals. The next year there were a few more. As time went on, the white peony turned almost entirely pink. That peony plant is still producing lovely flowers almost 50 years later, but it never produced pure white flowers again.

The peony plant lost its pure white color by being planted close enough to the pink one that the two plants could cross-pollinate. The darker color eventually won out. The slow but permanent change that took place also provides us with a graphic illustration of how our lives can be affected by those we choose to closely associate with. When we spend a significant amount of time with those who do share the same beliefs or values we have, over time the darker color can begin to win out by affecting our own attitudes. When God urged His people to "come out from them and be separate" (2 Cor. 6:17) His intent was not for us to become isolationists or to lock ourselves safely away in a closet. Though He told us that we are no longer of this world, He also chose to send us out into this world as His representatives. That's because the world needs white peonies. It needs those pure, untainted followers of God who are willing to get out there and show others how they can be white, too.

Berry Beautiful

Do not consider his appearance or his height, for I have rejected him. The LORD does not look at the things man looks at. Man looks at the outward appearance, but the LORD looks at the heart (1 Sam. 16:7).

A dear friend of mine had spent most of her life struggling with a bad self-image. Even knowing that God made her in His image and loved her just the way she was, she still found herself feeling ashamed of the way she looked. Something happened one day that gave her a whole new perspective on her problem. God spoke to her in a berry patch. She had gone to a commercial strawberry field to pick berries for her annual batch of jams that she gave out as Christmas gifts. At first, as she walked along the rows of plants she had trouble finding any berries at all. It was only after she bent down and looked under the leaves of the plants that she found they were literally teeming with strawberries. As she began filling her basket with the berries an encouraging thought came to mind, almost as if God himself was speaking directly to her. All of the luscious fruit she was finding had initially been completely hidden from sight. The very thing that made strawberry plants what they were and gave them their worth had nothing to do with what was seen at first glance.

My friend began to see herself as one of those strawberry plants. On first glance, she knew she would never be the one who turns heads with her great beauty when she enters a room. Yet, like the strawberries, God showed her that just below the surface was a much greater kind of beauty. He showed her how richly He had blessed her with many gifts and special talents (one I will gladly attest to is her strawberry jam). But even beyond that, He gave her the ability and desire to use those gifts to bless others. Truly, she has been given one of the most precious gifts of all. She has a loving heart — His heart, to be exact. So when she reaches out and loves others it is with the very heart of God. Nothing could be more beautiful than that.

The Evergreen Hedge

Have you not put a hedge around him and his house-hold and everything he has? You have blessed the work of his hands, so that his flocks and herds are spread throughout the land (Job 1:10).

We thought it would improve the scenery to have the old shed torn down. It had come with the house and, so we thought, was nothing but an eyesore. What we found instead was that when it was removed, our house was completely exposed to the apartment building next door, and the busy highway just behind it. We had never noticed any traffic noises while the shed was up but now heard them continually, day and night. Fortunately, the problem was easily solved and the end product better than I could have imagined. I planted a row of Canadian hemlock trees the entire length of the property, which grew into a solid hedge over the next few years. It wasn't until later that I discovered what an excellent choice I had unknowingly made in tree selection. In addition to blocking out sights and sounds, a tall evergreen hedge on the north side of the house can cut heating bills up to 34 percent in windy areas and even by 10 percent in sheltered areas. My lovely hedge would even protect us from the cold!

Considering all that a row of evergreens can do, it is no surprise that the Scriptures would use the illustration of a hedge to describe God's protective care of His children. Unlike seasonal bushes that leave one completely exposed for several months of the year, the evergreen hedge is a year-round, protective wall that continually blocks out undesirable noises, views, and the bitter chill of the winter winds. God never promised He would remove us from this troubled world but He did say He would protect us and keep us from all evil. As the Psalmist put it, "He is my loving God and my fortress, my stronghold and my deliverer, my shield, in whom I take refuge" (Ps. 144:2). I've often prayed for loved ones by asking the Lord to put a protective hedge around them. When I try to picture this hedge in my mind, it's always ever-green.

The Drought

He is like a tree planted by streams of water, which yields its fruit in season and whose leaf does not wither (Ps. 1:3).

It didn't rain in the month of June. I didn't worry much about it but did my best to keep my gardens well watered. But then, it didn't rain in July. I kept watering and my plants continued to grow. However, the lawn turned brown. When it didn't rain in August, I realized that although the gardens were just fine, several of the trees I had planted a few years earlier had dropped their needles and seemed to have died almost overnight. I was devastated. If only I had known that they needed water just as badly as the flowers and tomato plants! I had assumed that if they had survived years of dry summers and freezing winters they would have been able to handle virtually anything at this point. I was wrong.

As I dug up the dead trees and replaced them with new, healthy ones I promised myself I would not make this mistake again. Trees need water. It's just that simple. The psalm came to mind that states, "Blessed is the man (whose) . . . delight is in the law of the LORD, and on his law he meditates day and night. He is like a tree planted by streams of water, which yields its fruit in season and whose leaf does not wither. Whatever he does prospers" (Ps. 1:1–3). All that my trees would have needed to survive the drought was water. The tiny seedlings in my garden all thrived because I faithfully provided them with the water they needed. The Psalmist compares a well-watered tree to a soul that has found its sustenance in God and His word. Is your spirit experiencing a drought? Are you feeling spiritually parched today? Come, drink freely from the River of Life. All that you need to restore your soul can be found in God's Word. He has promised, "I will refresh the weary and satisfy the faint" (Jer. 31:25). I'll drink to that!

For in the day of trouble he will keep me safe in his dwelling; he will hide me in the shelter of his tabernacle and set me high upon a rock (Ps. 27:5).

You've probably heard the expression, "If you've got lemons, make lemonade." In the gardening world that might be adapted to, "If you've got rocks, make a rock garden." Rock gardens are designed to duplicate the natural environment in which rocks and mountain plants are found. Since the idea is to replicate nature, the rock garden is easier to manage than an ordinary garden. The plants used are generally hardier, more drought resistant and require less fertilizer than other plants. The rock garden is best suited for a slightly sloping, well-drained area such as a rocky hillside. Plants include flowering, hardy perennials, dwarf trees, and shrubs. And, of course, rocks! The rocks are usually laid on their larger edges so they appear natural. A few select larger rocks usually look better than a number of small ones. The rocks most commonly used in rock gardens are sandstone and limestone.

Making a rock garden out of a yard full of rocks is not just fun, it is also practical. While it turns an otherwise dead space into a thriving garden, it also helps prevent erosion. After all, what more solid foundation could a garden be built upon than rock? That is why God is often referred to as the Rock. The Psalmist wrote, "The LORD is my rock, my fortress and my deliverer; my God is my rock, in whom I take refuge" (Ps. 18:2). He is a source of stability and strength for all who entrust their lives to Him. It is like building one's house upon a rock. We read, "The rain came down, the streams rose, and the winds blew and beat against that house; yet it did not fall, because it had its foundation on the rock" (Matt. 7:25). Building upon rocks works for houses and for rock gardens. But building our lives upon Jesus comes with a full warranty. He is the "chosen and precious corner-stone, and the one who trusts in him will never be put to shame" (1 Pet. 2:6).

Growing Patience

Wait for the LORD and keep his way. He will exalt you to inherit the land (Ps. 37:34).

I had only seen its picture in gardening books but I recognized the wisteria plant the moment I saw it. It was every bit as lovely as I had envisioned it with its graceful branches covered with long, drooping flower clusters. As much as I love this magnificent specimen I have never attempted to grow one for two main reasons. First, I didn't know of anyone in our area who had successfully grown a wisteria plant and, second, I didn't know if I had enough patience. Wisteria will not bloom the first year it is planted. In fact, it has been known to take as many as seven years to bloom the first time. Wisteria is actually a climbing plant and a member of the legume family. It is often used to cover trellises or doorways but it can also be trained to carry its own weight and form a tree-like shape. If done properly a wisteria will grow up to ten feet and more, adding more stems and more feet of growth every year, ultimately becoming a spectacular, freestanding centerpiece.

Many of the best things in life come only with patience. This is as true in the spiritual realm as in the physical world. When we bring our requests to the Lord in prayer, we know He hears us and He always answers. Sometimes, however, His answer is, "Wait." If we trust Him even then, these can be the times of our greatest spiritual growth. God knows the process is sometimes even more worthwhile to us than the fulfillment of our request. It takes a lot of patience to grow wisteria but it is well worth the wait for this glorious flower-covered visual delight. Growing patience is also worth the wait. We will be listed among those the Bible describes as "those who through faith and patience inherit what has been promised" (Heb. 6:12). What God's children will one day inherit is far greater than whatever it was we were waiting for. Just be patient!

The Raised Bed

He lifted me out of the slimy pit, out of the mud and mire; he set my feet on a rock and gave me a firm place to stand (Ps. 40:2).

You've got the perfect spot for a garden except for that drainage problem? The solution for you might just be to build a raised garden. If your little spot happens to be a place where water tends to collect, or your soil has a heavy clay content, the raised bed will provide the plants with the additional drainage they need. Plus, since it doesn't require hauling in tons of soil, it isn't hard to do. Using landscape timber or stones, erect a short wall several inches high. After loosening the ground, fill the selected area with topsoil, peat moss, or compost. When the soil is mostly clay, add some sand, which will help loosen the clay and allow for proper drainage. Then, go ahead and plant that dream garden. You'll have your own little garden paradise before you know it.

God has planted each of us in our own perfect spot here on earth. Even there, spiritual growth is, at times, like trying to grow plants out of clay.

Troubles can seem to pour down like rain and, rather than drain away, only collect around us. At other times we find ourselves stuck in our own clay-like routines. However, the believer is like a plant growing in the raised bed. God did not promise to remove us from every difficult situation we face. Instead, He enables us to rise above it. Ironically, rising above initially requires bending down. We must admit our own inability to handle things and then "Humble yourselves before the Lord, and he will lift you up" (James 4:10). God will place anyone who humbly cries to Him for help in a raised bed high above their troubles. We are told, "The LORD upholds all those who fall and lifts up all who are bowed down (Ps. 145:14). As He does, our fears will simply drain away. And speaking of raised gardens, wait until you see the next one He's working on. You'll have your own spot in His garden paradise before you know it.

Succession Planting

Even when I am old and gray, do not forsake me, O God, till I declare your power to the next generation, your might to all who are to come (Ps. 71:18).

Even those who only have a tiny area for a garden can literally triple its productivity with a little creativity and careful planning. One of the most effective uses of garden space is accomplished by succession planting. Proper use of this technique will allow you to plant a succession of crops all in the same area. At the beginning of the season, plant the crops that mature early. Then, as soon as they have been harvested pull them up and have a second crop ready to go in the ground. This can be done by starting them ahead of time in peat pots. Once the second crop is harvested you may still have time for one more planting of cool weather crops. So, from that one small plot of land, you can enjoy an entire season's worth of produce.

God's church has been growing and producing fruit for almost 2,000 years now. Here, on this tiny globe He has faithfully maintained His garden of growing believers and has done it using His own version of succession planting. His success is due, in part, to each of us carrying out our part in passing the word on to the next generation. As the Psalmist explains, "We will not hide them from their children; we will tell the next generation the praiseworthy deeds of the LORD, his power, and the wonders he has done. He decreed statutes for Jacob and established the law in Israel, which he commanded our forefathers to teach their children, so the next generation would know them, even the children yet to be born, and they in turn would tell their children" (Ps. 78:4–6). As in maintaining any garden, it hasn't always been easy. Throughout the centuries the Church has faced an unending barrage of hardships, opposition, persecution, and even martyrdom. Despite it all, the Master Gardener made certain His people not only survive but thrive, and will continue to do so right up until the final harvest.

Evergreen or Deciduous

The righteous will flourish like a palm tree, they will grow like a cedar of Lebanon (Ps. 92:12).

I was delighted to get her letter but was shocked when I discovered all my friend had gone through since I had last seen her. She described her divorce, the custody battles over her children, a list of health problems, and on top of it all, the loss of her job. It was no wonder, under such a heavy load, that her faith in God had nearly crumbled. Then this dear friend, who happens to have a master's degree in forestry, ended her letter by comparing the two of us to trees. She wrote, "Your faith has always been evergreen and mine will always be deciduous. Why can't I be more like you?" She was referring to the fact that, while evergreens retain their needles throughout the year, the deciduous tree changes with the seasons and sheds all its leaves when winter comes. The word "deciduous" literally means short-lived or temporary.

I pulled out a pen and paper and wrote back to my friend urging her to hang on tightly to the God who loves her so very much. Then I reminded her of some of the difficult times I had been through and how I, too, had experienced having a deciduous faith. Though I had tried desperately to trust Him in the trials, there were times when my ability to do so simply failed me. But it was at that very point that God spoke to me through what has become one of my favorite promises. The Bible assures us that "if we are faithless, he will remain faithful, for he cannot disown himself" (2 Tim. 2:13). When we have committed our lives to God's care, He will not let go of us even when we are unable to hold on to Him. It's okay to be deciduous now and then. Winters will come, but they are short-lived. Spring will always follow bringing new life, new growth and a new faith well on the way to becoming evergreen.

They will still bear fruit in old age, they will stay fresh and green (Ps. 92:14).

Many of the most beautiful garden flowers one can grow are perennials. Even better, as the name indicates, perennials grow back every year. *Perennial* literally means lasting throughout the years, lasting indefinitely, or perpetual. Some of the most popular perennials include bleeding hearts, chrysanthemums, English daisies, foxgloves, hibiscus, hollyhocks, peonies, roses, and sweet Williams. While the perennial plant will die back each year, the underground part lives through the winter and springs forth with new shoots in the following growing season. With proper care, these flowers will grow bigger, stronger, and more beautiful with every passing season. Some even spread and multiply. Unlike annuals that come and go with a single blaze of glory and are gone, perennials offer a lifetime of color to your garden.

We have all seen people like those lovely annuals who seem to come to a faith in God in a burst of dramatic color. But at some point, something happens. Their enthusiasm wanes and eventually fades away altogether. What started as a blaze of glory is gone almost as fast as it began. There are others, however, who come to believe in God, quietly at first, but soon begin to grow. As time goes by, rather than ebbing, their faith steadily continues to grow. Years later these believers will not only be strong in their faith but will have inspired others by their example. What they have is truly a perennial faith that no one could question because, as the Scriptures state, "Thus, by their fruit you will recognize them" (Matt. 7:20). Their strength lies in that they are not dependent on their own fragile, "annual" human emotions to carry them through the difficult seasons of life, but on the perennial faithfulness of God. How long does that last? He assures us, "Even to your old age and gray hairs I am he, I am he who will sustain you. I have made you and I will carry you; I will sustain you and I will rescue you" (Isa. 46:4). Now that's perennial!

Standing Firm

Blessed is the man you discipline, O LORD, the man you teach from your law; you grant him relief from days of trouble (Ps. 94:12–13).

My new tree came with a complete set of instructions. Some of them I followed meticulously. Others I chose to ignore, including the suggestion to stake a young tree. A few days later, I looked out the window during a rather brisk wind and noticed my new tree being violently whipped around. I was suddenly inspired with a renewed interest in following directions. Staking, I learned, is for the protection and proper training of a new tree or shrub, specifically in regard to wind damage. Right then, wind and all, I went out and staked the new tree, carefully following each step in the instructions. I hammered a strong two to three foot stake into the ground approximately eight to ten inches from the trunk of the tree. I made sure it was on the side from which the strongest winds blow (which I had no difficulty deciphering at that moment). I tied the tree to the stake with soft twine to prevent injury to the trunk. While not all trees need staking, it is advised for many-branched shade trees as well as young trees in an unprotected area. The next time I looked out the window I saw my new tree standing strong despite the wind.

There are times when we need a little extra staking to stand up against life's stormy winds. Once staked, my little tree was held firmly in place and was protected from being blown whichever way the wind was going. Because of His great love for us, the Lord sometimes reaches out His hand and stops us from going in a certain direction we were headed in. At the time, that may feel a bit like being staked but we are told, "My son, do not despise the LORD's discipline and do not resent his rebuke, because the LORD disciplines those he loves, as a father the son he delights in" (Prov. 3:11). God's discipline is our security. He loves us enough to stake us so that when the winds blow we'll be standing firm.

Hardy Mums

I was pushed back and about to fall, but the LORD helped me. The LORD is my strength and my song; he has become my salvation (Ps. 118:13–14).

It is a sure sign of autumn when the hardy mums start to appear. After a season of summer blooms, suddenly everywhere one looks the impatiens and petunias are replaced with pots full of fall mums. Chrysanthemums are short day plants, meaning they require long periods of uninterrupted darkness for the flower buds to develop. That is why they don't bloom until fall when the hours of daylight have decreased. The hardy mum is the obvious favorite for fall gardeners because, unlike most other flowers that wilt as soon as the cold weather arrives, it continues to thrive sometimes even as the first snowflakes are falling. As its name indicates, this popular perennial is, indeed, hardy and usually survives the cold winter months to show its magnificent colors again the following season.

Seeing those bright flowers flourishing despite the falling temperatures makes me ask myself if I hold up as well when the going gets tough. When adversities hit me like a blast of wintry air, do I find myself withering like a summer petunia or do I stand firm and show my colors like the hardy mum? While I admit to a little of both, I have learned that the secret to spiritual hardiness is not achieved by trying to tough it out in our own strength. It's not who I am that will get me through the wintry trials, but who I am relying on. The Bible tells us, "Do not be afraid. Stand firm and you will see the deliverance the LORD will bring you today. . . . The LORD will fight for you; you need only to be still" (Exod. 14:13–14). While some will continue to struggle along, trying to make it through life on their own, "We trust in the name of the LORD our God. They are brought to their knees and fall, but we rise up and stand firm" (Ps. 20:7–8). If the Lord is my source of strength then even during the most difficult seasons of life, mum's the word!

The Lilac Grove

Where there is no vision, the people perish
(Prov. 29:18;KJV).

It was a deal I couldn't pass up. The mail order catalog was offering six lilac plants for $10.00. We were on a tight budget but I had always dreamed of having my very own lilac grove. Knowing it would take years to grow, I wanted to get started as soon as possible so I dropped my check in the mail immediately. The plants would be shipped in time for the spring planting season. My husband was with me when they arrived several weeks later. When I saw the small padded envelope I was confused. I carefully opened it and pulled out what looked like six brown sticks. "Whatever they are, they look dead," my husband commented, obviously holding back a chuckle. But my initial disappointment quickly faded away when I read a small note enclosed with the plants explaining that bare-rooted plants might look dead but are guaranteed to be healthy. I smiled at my husband and replied, "They're not dead. They're my lilac grove." Now that took faith, but by the end of the summer

I had six healthy plants and within the next few years I had my lilac grove.

Like those dead-looking lilac plants, before we invite the Lord into our lives every one of us "were dead in your transgressions and sins" (Eph. 2:1). But where He saw death, God also saw potential. We are told, "Because of his great love for us, God, who is rich in mercy, made us alive with Christ even when we were dead in transgressions — it is by grace you have been saved. And God raised us up with Christ and seated us with him in the heavenly realms in Christ Jesus (Eph. 2:4–6). Now that takes faith, but if we will place our life in His care, we can become a permanent living transplant in His kingdom. If sticks can be turned into a lilac grove, just imagine what God can do with a life entrusted to Him. Or, better yet, try it for yourself.

I am a rose of Sharon, a lily of the valleys
(Song of Sol. 2:1).

I had heard the old hymn countless times before: "Jesus, Rose of Sharon, bloom within my heart; Beauties of Thy truth and holiness impart, That where'er I go my life may shed abroad. Fragrance of the knowledge of the love of God" (Ida A. Guirey, circa 1922). It wasn't until I started gardening that I began to wonder why the hymn writer had chosen the Rose of Sharon. The modern-day Rose of Sharon is an ornamental shrub also called the *Hibiscus syriacus*. It is an upright deciduous shrub with bell-shaped rose, violet, or white single and double flowers that resemble hollyhock blossoms. At maturity it reaches 10–12 feet tall and 6 feet wide. When I looked the Rose of Sharon up in a gardening book I learned that the name has also been applied to other plants. It stated that the biblical Rose of Sharon made famous in the Song of Solomon has not been identified but is believed by some botanists to be a species of narcissus or crocus.

How, then, did this crocus-like flower come to be associated with the name of Jesus? The answer is found in the Book of Isaiah, which describes Sharon as a desert plain, then states, "The wilderness and the solitary place shall be glad for them; and the desert shall rejoice, and blossom as the rose. It shall blossom abundantly, and rejoice even with joy and singing . . . the excellency of Carmel and Sharon, they shall see the glory of the Lord, and the excellency of our God" (Isa. 35:1–2;KJV). Isaiah was prophesying the coming of the long-awaited Messiah, comparing the event to a flower blooming in the desert. Or, in modern terms, to a crocus popping out of the snow in early spring.

Indeed, all of the prophecies were fulfilled in Jesus. As the hymn writer put it, "Jesus, Rose of Sharon, sweeter far to see. Than the fairest flow'rs of earth could ever be, Fill my life completely, adding more each day Of Thy grace divine and purity, I pray."

Faux Winter

Arise, my darling, my beautiful one, and come with me. See! The winter is past; the rains are over and gone (Song of Sol. 2:10–11).

No matter how early I plant seeds in the spring, it always seems like too long a wait until the first flowers actually bloom. I came across an article one day that offered some very creative solutions to speeding up the germination process. Natural seeds go through a dormant stage. Last year's flowers delay germination until spring so they will have the maximum time to grow before having to survive their first winter. One way to speed up the process is to put them through a "faux winter" as the article put it, explaining that it isn't really necessary for the seed to spend the cold months in the ground, as long as it *thinks* it did. The article suggested placing the seeds in a small container with moist sand or peat, and leaving them in the refrigerator for 4-6 weeks. The seeds will think it is winter, come out of dormancy, and before you know it, you'll have flowers.

Many of us go through periods of dormancy.

Whether it is due to discouragement, depression, complacency, or even backsliding in our faith, we become stagnant in our spiritual growth. Like those dormant seeds, God knows that for us to experience life to the fullest we need to be woken up and that may take a bit of faux winter. Yet, what may seem like wintry trials is a loving Father's wake-up call. We are told, "My son, do not make light of the Lord's discipline, and do not lose heart when he rebukes you, because the Lord disciplines those he loves, and he punishes everyone he accepts as a son" (Heb. 12:5–6). Like an icy shock to the dormant seeds, "God disciplines us for our good, that we may share in his holiness. No discipline seems pleasant at the time, but painful. Later on, however, it produces a harvest of righteousness and peace for those who have been trained by it" (Heb. 12:10–11). So, "Wake up, O sleeper, rise from the dead, and Christ will shine on you" (Eph. 5:14).

Their root shall be as rottenness, and their blossom shall go up as dust (Isa. 5:24;KJV).

I admit I asked for it. I was getting pretty tired of having to lug bucket after bucket of water every night to each of my gardens. It had been an unusually dry summer, so it was either that or watch all my flowers shrivel up and die. I yelled out to my neighbor as she, too, was out faithfully watering her garden, "Hey, do you know any rain dances?" The next day, before either of us did any dancing, it began to rain. No, it began to pour. I was ecstatic. *A night off*, I thought gleefully. The next day it continued to rain. Then the day after that. In fact, it rained for a week. I realized one of my gardens was not just watered; it was under water. The backyard was flooded. When the rain finally stopped, it was too late. The flowers had drooped down and eventually fell off the dead and rotting plants. I guess they just got too much of a good thing.

The Bible describes a scene of rotting plants that sounds similar to my ruined garden but there is great consolation to be found in this passage. We live in a fallen world. Evil people do terrible things and often appear to go unpunished while innocent victims remain unavenged. In reality, God sees it all and has declared, "Woe to those who call evil good and good evil, who put darkness for light and light for darkness . . . who acquit the guilty for a bribe, but deny justice to the innocent . . . so their roots will decay and their flowers blow away like dust; for they have rejected the law of the LORD Almighty"(Isa. 5:20–24). In the garden, it is water that sustains life. Yet, when torrential floods pour down, they can claim life. In mankind, it is our Lord who sustains life. However, when His holy wrath is poured upon the unrepentant, that evilness will be purged. God will avenge His children. They will watch and see what happens when bad people experience too much of a Good thing.

The wolf will live with the lamb, the leopard will lie down with the goat, the calf and the lion and the yearling together; and a little child will lead them (Isa. 11:6).

The moment I saw them, I was determined to have some lupines of my own some day. It ended up being that very day. I stopped at a gardening store on the way home and before the sun had set, my lupine seeds were planted. Lupines are perennials producing spikes of pea-like flowers. These magnificent specimens come in a wide assortment of colors and are easy to identify by their palmate leaves and the pea-shaped flowers. Lupines are members of the bean or Fabaceae (*fab* meaning "bean" in Latin) family. The bean family provides some of mankind's most nutritious food crops such as soybeans, fababeans, chick peas, and legumes such as alfalfa and clover. However, it also produces a wide variety of toxins. The lupine, despite its breathtaking beauty, contains high levels of toxic alkaloids. The name lupine comes from the Latin *lupus* for wolf, given in ancient times because of an old belief that the plants destroy the soul.

Jesus used the illustration of a wolf to describe our spiritual enemies saying, "I am the good shepherd. The good shepherd lays down his life for the sheep . . . the wolf attacks the flock and scatters it" (John 10:11–12). He warned us, "They come to you in sheep's clothing, but inwardly they are ferocious wolves" (Matt. 7:15). It was also originally believed that lupines somehow stole nutrients from the soil. We now know the opposite to be true. Though lupines are not edible, they are, nevertheless, an important agricultural crop, helping the soil by building up nitrogen and by stabilizing it with their deep roots. So the original fears about lupines that earned them their name were unfounded. They neither destroy the soil nor the soul. The Bible uses the wolf to signify our enemies, but it also describes a day when even they need no longer be feared. In that day we are told that the wolf will lay down with the lamb. We will see all our enemies, both natural and supernatural, bow themselves to the Good Shepherd.

Labyrinths

Whether you turn to the right or to the left, your ears will hear a voice behind you, saying, "This is the way; walk in it" (Isa. 30:21).

When I was a little girl my parents took me to Colonial Williamsburg, an old-style village complete with people in original colonial dress. What stood out most to me, even as a child, was the impeccably kept grounds. Throughout the village the gardens, planted in an authentic colonial style, were meticulously cared for. The one I enjoyed most was the garden maze. Garden mazes, also called labyrinths, are passages walled by clipped hedges. They are life-sized mazes in which people attempt to find their way through the many passageways and out the other end. There is only one correct path and I remember taking quite a few wrong turns and dead ends (and if I were to be completely honest, one shortcut) before I finally found my way out.

The term labyrinth was also used to describe the mazelike patterns on the floors of some medieval churches to symbolize the tortuous journey of Christian pilgrims. For many of us life, indeed, is like a labyrinth. We continually have to choose which path to take and often the answer is unclear. God knew of the difficult choices we would face, and promised He would guide us all the way through if we let Him. He promised, "Along unfamiliar paths I will guide them; I will turn the darkness into light before them and make the rough places smooth. These are the things I will do; I will not forsake them" (Isa. 42:16). Eventually, He will lead us out of the maze altogether. As the Psalmist wrote, "You guide me with your counsel, and afterward you will take me into glory" (Ps. 73:24). The path to glory is one choice God made perfectly clear. When asked, "How can we know the way?" Jesus answered, "I am the way and the truth and the life. No one comes to the Father except through me" (John 14:6). Jesus is the direct route through the maze. Oh, and there *will* be a prize at the end of the course.

Like birds hovering overhead, the LORD Almighty will shield Jerusalem; he will shield it and deliver it, he will "pass over" it and will rescue it (Isa. 31:5).

After yanking the last weed from my garden I stood to my feet and pulled out my red bandana. I wiped a smudge of dirt off my face as I proudly inspected my work. Suddenly, I heard a low-pitched buzzing noise right behind me. I turned to find myself face to face with a tiny hummingbird hanging frozen in midair. I stood spellbound as this tiny flying machine hovered motionlessly before me, apparently as fascinated by me as I was with him. Though the whole encounter lasted only a few seconds it seemed that time momentarily stopped as the two of us investigated each other.

Hummingbirds are intensely inquisitive despite their minute size. They are the smallest of all birds, weighing about 8 ounces. Nevertheless, they are quite bold, and fiercely territorial. They also readily become accustomed to humans and will swoop down to investigate red clothing. Some of the tiniest species of hummingbirds have a wing beat of 80 per second, traveling up to 60 mph, and need to feed about every ten minutes all day long. They hover in the air to feed from flowers, using their long, tapered bills to probe inside for their nectar, which they consume at about 13 licks a second. This is, no doubt, why in Portuguese they are called *beija-flor,* meaning "kiss-flower." They are the only birds that can fly backwards and do this to move away from the flowers. As they feed, hummers accidentally collect pollen, and in moving from flower to flower they help the flowers to reproduce. This amazing little creature is a living testimony to the wonder of its Maker. The Bible uses the illustration of a bird "hovering overhead" to describe the Lord's active involvement in our lives (Isa. 31:5). Like the hummingbird, He remains fixed in place as our shield and defender. He, too, is bold and fiercely territorial especially when it comes to looking out for His children so there is no place where we are more secure than under His protective wings.

Wildflowers

All men are like grass, and all their glory is like the flowers of the field. . . . The grass withers and the flowers fall, but the word of our God stands forever (Isa. 40:6–8).

As much as I enjoy gardening, I do enjoy taking weekends off. We spend weekends at our little cabin in the wilderness where we just sit back and enjoy the beautiful, natural landscaping. For me, that means no planting, weeding, or watering. However, that hasn't stopped us from enjoying a fresh bouquet of flowers on the table every week. Our property is surrounded by fields and meadows filled with some of the loveliest wildflowers I have ever seen. When I look at some of these magnificent centerpieces I realize that my best gardening efforts could not have produced anything more beautiful than what is already growing in the wild. But that really shouldn't come as a surprise. We humans may be able to design some lovely gardens but we aren't the ones who created flowers. Before mankind even arrived on the scene God was in the gardening business, but He started from scratch.

So, whether purchased at the local garden store or grown in the wild, the credit for all floral beauty truly goes to Him.

That's good news for us. The Scriptures explain, "See how the lilies of the field grow. They do not labor or spin. Yet I tell you that not even Solomon in all his splendor was dressed like one of these. If that is how God clothes the grass of the field, which is here today and tomorrow is thrown into the fire, will he not much more clothe you?" (Matt. 6:28–30). The Creator of the universe is intimately involved in every detail of this world but His concern about wildflowers can't compare to the love He has for us. If we can trust Him to fill the earth with such color and beauty, how much more can we trust Him with our daily needs, concerns, and even our very lives? Those wildflowers on the table are not just a reprieve from gardening. They are a reminder of a loving provider who never takes time off from His garden, or from me.

Supernatural Strength

Those who hope in the LORD will renew their strength. They will soar on wings like eagles; they will run and not grow weary, they will walk and not be faint (Isa. 40:31).

I learned something about trees that I wouldn't have believed if I hadn't heard it from a forestry school. It has been shown that some of the hardiest trees on this earth can actually withstand temperatures much colder than ever occur naturally. This was proven by collecting branches of a cold-climate tree and immersing it in liquid nitrogen, which maintains a temperature of -196°C. Though the branches reached -196°C almost instantly, they survived.

It was explained that certain hardy plants' winter cells are so dry that there is no water available inside them to form ice. Since it is ice and not the low temperature that kills the plant, even liquid nitrogen can't kill them. That means the coldest climates on this planet are no match for these hardy trees. God certainly knew what He was doing when He designed certain plants with an almost supernatural ability to endure the most extreme conditions . . . and beyond.

God also knew what He was doing when He sent His followers out into what, at times, would be a harsh and hostile world. He told us right up front that things would get tough now and then, but He also assured us that we were thoroughly equipped to handle anything that occurs naturally and, in fact, much more. The Bible warns us that we have spiritual enemies in this world and that "our struggle is not against flesh and blood, but against the rulers, against the authorities, against the powers of this dark world and against the spiritual forces of evil in the heavenly realms" (Eph. 6:12). However, that warning is immediately followed with the assurance that with God's help we are invincible. We need only to "put on the full armor of God, so that when the day of evil comes, you may be able to stand your ground, and after you have done everything, to stand" (Eph. 6:13). Like those hardy branches, we can handle even the most extreme conditions and far beyond because our source of strength is, indeed, supernatural.

The Legend of the Dogwood

But he was pierced for our transgressions, he was crushed for our iniquities; the punishment that brought us peace was upon him, and by his wounds we are healed (Isa. 53:5).

Its fragrant blossoms appear even before its leaves, offering the winter-weary world a sure sign of the new season. The dogwood tree flowers in early spring with tiny, greenish-yellow flowers clustered in the center of four white or pinkish petals. Most species of dogwoods are small trees or shrubs with simple leaves, but a few species, including the flowering dogwood, are popular for their ornamental value. Many songbirds and animals eat the fruit of the dogwood, and its wood is used in making furniture. In the fall, it again boldly proclaims the new season with its show of brilliant red leaves.

The reappearance of blossoms on the dogwood tree is a proclamation of the arrival of spring. But if one were to look just a bit closer, as legend has it, those blossoms have another message to deliver. According to the legend, in the days of

Christ the dogwood tree originally grew to be the same size as the oak tree and other monarchs of the forest. Because of its great size and strength the dogwood was the tree used to make the cross Jesus was crucified on. The mighty tree was greatly distressed at having to be used to kill its own Maker, and Jesus, now resurrected, sensed this. Because of His great care for the suffering and pain of any of His creations He told the tree, "Because of your anguish over My suffering and death, I will cause the dogwood tree to never grow large enough again to be used as a cross. Henceforth, it will be slender, bent, and twisted and its blossoms will be in the form of a cross with two long and two short petals. In the center of the outer edge of each petal there will be nail prints, brown with rust and stained with red, and in the center of the flower will be a crown of thorns, and all who see this will remember." When you see the dogwood's lovely blossoms next spring, be sure to remember.

Which Came First?

The rain and the snow come down from heaven, and do not return to it without watering the earth and making it bud and flourish, so that it yields seed for the sower and bread for the eater (Isa. 55:10).

Which came first, the plant or the seed? This question is reminiscent of the "chicken or the egg" debates many of us had in school. You start with a seed and end up with a plant. But then, where did the seed come from? The answer always seemed obvious to me. They both came from the grocery store. (I would point out that I didn't do very well in science class.)

The "which came first" question is commonly posed to get us thinking about how life began, but to me, it was a waste of time. I was fortunate enough to have learned as a child that seeds, plants, chickens, and eggs all came from the same source. God made them. While far greater minds than mine continue to ponder how life began, I know that "In the beginning was the Word, and the Word was with God, and the Word was God. . . . Through him all things were made;

without him nothing was made that has been made" (John 1:1–3). It doesn't get much simpler than that.

Now the Bible offers some advice to those who are serious about finding the ultimate answer to life. It says to "Seek the LORD while he may be found; call on him while he is near. Let the wicked forsake his way and the evil man his thoughts. Let him turn to the LORD, and he will have mercy on him, and to our God, for he will freely pardon. . . . As the heavens are higher than the earth, so are my ways higher than your ways and my thoughts than your thoughts" (Isa. 55:6–9). The thoughts of God are truly far above any of our own, but He chose to share some of them with us through His word. As the rain causes both seeds and plants to grow, His word will accomplish everything He sent it to do. That includes revealing himself to us, along with providing answers to enough of our questions that we can trust Him with the rest.

Mutations

Instead of their shame my people will receive a double portion, and instead of disgrace they will rejoice in their inheritance; and so they will inherit a double portion in their land, and everlasting joy will be theirs (Isa. 61:7).

According to plant breeders, what exists today can be made even better tomorrow. One of the ways they attempt to improve plants is by constantly being on the lookout for a break or mutation. In a field where thousands of the same species of flowers are growing, trained eyes may spot one with a different color. This unique plant could be a mutation that can be developed into a new variety. A mutation is an abrupt, spontaneous departure from the normal hereditary pattern. Mutations can happen in one of two ways. They can be natural or artificial mutations. As its name indicates, a natural mutation occurs with no intervention from mankind. An artificial mutation is caused by treating plants with certain chemicals. In 1956 the world's first atomic-bred flower was developed by subjecting a carnation with red spots to gamma rays. The radiation eliminated the spots creating an artificially mutated pure white carnation.

On occasion, humans go through sudden mutations. In plant breeders' terms, these drastic changes can be either artificial or natural mutations. When someone faces the sudden loss of a loved one, is abused by another person, or goes through some other kind of devastating event they can be so deeply effected that their personality abruptly changes, sometimes for the rest of their life. This is an artificial or manmade mutation. But there is another event that occurs in people's lives that causes a natural mutation. One simple act of faith on the part of an individual can, indeed, cause an abrupt departure from their normal hereditary patterns "and into an inheritance that can never perish, spoil or fade — kept in heaven for you" (1 Pet. 1:4). This mutation may seem spontaneous on our part but in reality, "He chose us in him before the creation of the world. . . . In love he predestined us to be adopted as his sons through Jesus Christ" (Eph. 1:4–5). One act of faith changes our lives forever. It's sudden, but it's only natural since He's been planning it all along.

I will cleanse them from all the sin they have committed against me and will forgive all their sins of rebellion against me (Jer. 33:8).

There's a jingle that our local radio station frequently uses as a public service announcement that starts, "Plant a tree for your tomorrow. It's a tree that clears the air. . . ." The tune is so catchy that it makes one want to go out and buy a tree which is, of course, the point of the advertisement. However, the message behind the music is indeed based on facts. It is a fact that one acre of trees has the ability to remove up to 13 tons of pollutants, in the form of particles and gases, from the air annually. Even smaller plants such as shrubs and lawns help to remove dust, smoke, and other pollution-causing agents from the air. It is also a fact that just one single tree can remove 26 pounds of carbon dioxide from the atmosphere annually, which is equivalent to 11,000 miles of car emissions. So the song is right. One tree really can make a difference. All it takes is one person willing to plant it.

History has proven time and again that one person really can make a difference. Look at any great accomplishment, any medical breakthrough, any scientific advancement or humanitarian mission and you'll find the vision of one person behind it. We humans have been given the capacity to accomplish virtually anything we put our minds to. The only problem mankind can't overcome is our own mortality. We can enhance our lives and, in some cases, even prolong them, but eventually each of us will face death. So, what no mortal man could do God did for us. He came to earth to make the ultimate difference. By giving His own life on our behalf He paid the debt for our sins once and for all, and in so doing, conquered death. One tree can go a long way in cleaning the air we breathe. One man, Jesus Christ, went the entire way in cleaning the sin-covered slate of mankind. And He did it on a tree.

I will give them an undivided heart and put a new spirit in them; I will remove from them their heart of stone and give them a heart of flesh (Ezek. 11:19).

Don't eat the leaves, we were warned. Though I had no intention of nibbling on the flower arrangement before me, I had to at least ask why. I learned that foxgloves are extremely poisonous. These gorgeous biennial flowers are members of the snapdragon family. Their tall spikes of beautiful bell-like flowers in pink, blue, or mauve, with dark spots inside the lip make them favorites of many gardeners. They are also the pharmaceutical source of the heart drug digitalis, which is poisonous in overdose. The key ingredient, digitoxin, is a glycoside used to stimulate the heart. A carefully prescribed dose often has a miraculous effect on people with heart conditions, but an overdose can be fatal.

The Bible tells us that all of mankind has a heart condition and that if left untreated it is quite fatal. We are told, "As for you, you were dead in your transgressions and sins" (Eph. 2:1). That is why God provided us with a miracle cure. It, too, came from a Living Plant. Prophecies of the coming of Christ stated that "In that day the Branch of the LORD will be beautiful and glorious, and the fruit of the land will be the pride and glory of the survivors in Israel" (Isa. 4:2). It was prophesied that "A shoot will come up from the stump of Jesse; from his roots a Branch will bear fruit" (Isa. 11:1). Jesus is that righteous branch and was planted here on earth to bring us the cure for our heart disease. He didn't just stimulate our hearts, however. He offered us a complete heart transplant saying, "I will give you a new heart and put a new spirit in you; I will remove from you your heart of stone and give you a heart of flesh" (Ezek. 36:26). The results are the same after every operation He performs. God "made us alive with Christ even when we were dead in transgressions — it is by grace you have been saved" (Eph. 2:4–5). Now that's a miracle cure!

The Right Mix

It had been planted in good soil by abundant water so that it would produce branches, bear fruit and become a splendid vine (Ezek. 17:8).

In choosing what flower to plant in a particular location three important factors must be taken into consideration: sunlight, soil content, and moisture level. First, one must be aware of the amount of sunlight this spot gets each day. Some plants require full sunlight while others thrive in the shade. Soil content cannot be neglected either. Soil is made up of any combination of sand, silt, and clay. Though plant preferences vary, a good balance of all three generally works best. Finally, one must keep in mind the level of moisture in that specific area. Is it too dry? Is there proper drainage? One quickly learns it is futile to try to grow plants in a place where the conditions are not right. A healthy, thriving garden always has the right combination of light, soil, and moisture.

To grow spiritually we, too, require the right kind of environment. First, we need ample exposure to the Light. Jesus is "the true light that gives light to every man" (John 1:9). Through spending time with Him in His Word we will get all the light we need. Having good soil to grow in comes from how we spend our time on this earth. A healthy balance of work and play is important, but it is essential to our spiritual growth that we also spend time in worship and in fellowship with other believers. We need each other to grow in our faith so how we invest our time directly effects whether our spiritual lives thrive or wither. If we take care of these first two areas, we can leave the watering to Him. God has promised those who seek Him that "He will lead them to springs of living water" (Rev. 7:17). Jesus reaffirmed that "whoever drinks the water I give him will never thirst. Indeed, the water I give him will become in him a spring of water welling up to eternal life" (John 4:14). With that kind of water source we can't help but thrive.

Ask the LORD for rain in the springtime; it is the LORD who makes the storm clouds. He gives showers of rain to men, and plants of the field to everyone (Zech. 10:1).

I used to think of rain showers as nothing more than an uninvited interruption to my vacation. Since I started gardening, my attitude toward rain has changed dramatically. While the modern weather forecasters sound almost apologetic when they predict a week of rain, it wasn't all that long ago that adequate rainfall was literally a matter of life and death. That was certainly the case during Bible times. People were utterly dependent on their crops to live, so rain was considered a blessing from the Lord. The opposite was true, as well. When droughts plagued the land it was seen as God's curse upon them. So what did they do when they desperately needed rain? They went directly to the source. We read, "Do any of the worthless idols of the nations bring rain? Do the skies themselves send down showers? No, it is you, O LORD our God. Therefore our hope is in you, for you are the one who does all this" (Jer. 14:22).

Today, most of us are far removed from feeling dependent on the rains to eat. Most of us have steady nine-to-five office jobs and take home weekly paychecks. Our main source of food is the grocery store. What do we care if it rains? Even modern farmers, with their agricultural advances, are better able to keep their gardens watered during times of drought. Despite the perception that we are able to provide for ourselves we are, in reality, just as dependent on God as ever. The Bible tells us that Jesus is "sustaining all things by his powerful word" (Heb. 1:3) and that "in him all things hold together" (Col. 1:17). That includes the earth, the sun, and every star in the universe. It also includes me. As the Psalmist wrote, "I lie down and sleep; I wake again, because the LORD sustains me" (Ps. 3:5). So bring on those showers. They keep my garden watered and remind me of the One from whom all blessings flow.

Jesus said to him, "Away from me, Satan! For it is written: 'Worship the Lord your God, and serve him only' " (Matt. 4:10).

Each year when we close our camp we wonder how many of the trees we planted will still be there in the spring. The answer lies in the deer population for the year. With an overabundance of deer, by the end of a hard winter virtually every tree within reach will have been stripped clean. When I tried to research the problem I found dozens of articles written by experts on the subject of deer repellents. Suggested remedies included everything from chemical sprays and electric fences to mothballs or human hair. My favorite, by far, was lion dung (though I'm not sure where one might purchase this product). On a more practical level, one article suggested hanging bars of soap from strings in the trees one wants to protect, two or three bars to a tree. The author writes, "The tree looks trashed, but the deer tend to stay away." Perhaps they agree with the author and have no interest in trees that looked trashed.

There are times in our lives when we find ourselves in serious need of some kind of repellent in the spiritual battles we fight. Temptations eat away at us like deer nibbling at trees and if we don't find a remedy our willpower will eventually be completely stripped away. To find the help we need we must go to the experts for advice. There is no better source, of course, than Jesus himself. While here on earth He fought the ultimate battle with the chief tempter and in so doing demonstrated to us how it is done. The primary tool He used to overcome Satan's temptations was the Bible. Satan tried to entice Jesus with offers of physical satisfaction, prestige, and power. Each time Jesus immediately responded by quoting Scriptures. After three tries Satan gave up and left in defeat. The Word of God was as unappealing to the devil as soap bars are to deer. That's why it should be our repellent of choice in every encounter we face with the enemy.

The Solar Light

In the same way, let your light shine before men, that they may see your good deeds and praise your Father in heaven (Matt. 5:16).

I discovered it in the garden section. I was looking for a light for my garden. There were plenty to choose from but most required wiring, outlets, and more work than I wanted to put into the project. Then I found something called a solar light. The concept was intriguing. The light has a large panel on its top that absorbs sunlight throughout the day, which charges the batteries. It has a light-sensitive switch so it comes on automatically at dusk, fully powered by solar light. How could I resist! I got all the pieces assembled, placed the batteries in the lid, and then stuck my solar lamp in the ground by the garden. Twelve hours later just after sunset, as if on cue, the light popped on. It was not the brightest light I had ever seen, but that little lantern glowed from the time it first came on (around 8:00 P.M.) throughout the rest of the night. It continued to do so, every night, for the rest of the season, faithfully producing just enough light to safely guide someone to the garden even in the darkest night.

As I sat and watched my little light glowing by the garden it reminded me of how the Bible refers to us as lights. Jesus told His followers, "You are the light of the world" (Matt. 5:14). He told them to go out into this dark world and bring it light. But He didn't expect them to do it in their own strength. No, He said, "I am the light of the world. Whoever follows me will never walk in darkness, but will have the light of life" (John 8:12). When He sends us out we have already been provided with all the light we'll ever need — that of himself. Like my solar light, we need only soak up the light He has poured down upon us. Then, when the darkness comes, we will shine with the light of His love. We don't need to light up the whole world — just enough to guide others to our light source.

Disappointments

Where your treasure is, there your heart will be also
(Matt. 6:21).

Last year I decided to use mixed flower seeds instead of buying plants for the two flowerpots at camp. Things started out fine. After a few weeks the tiny shoots appeared. Then came the drought. Since I could only water on the weekends, I soon lost several of the young plants. Then came the windstorm. We arrived one week to find both pots blown upside-down. By late July only two plants remained, both marigolds, one in each pot. "Why don't you just go buy some geraniums?" my husband suggested, but I was determined to succeed. By late August, the two plants began to show promise. I could almost taste success. It wasn't until September that the first signs of flower heads began to appear. One week before camp closing, I knew the time had arrived. We would surely have lovely marigolds to greet us the following week and my labors would not be in vain. When we arrived a week later I ran to my flowerpots with camera in hand to capture this exciting moment on film. As fate would have it, during the week a deer had come along and chomped the heads off of both plants.

It is easy to get caught up in certain projects or activities. Sometimes we can be so consumed by them that they become an obsession. But if the object of our passion somehow fails us we can be left quite devastated. That's why the Scriptures urge us, "Do not store up for yourselves treasures on earth, where moth and rust destroy, and where thieves break in and steal. But store up for yourselves treasures in heaven. . . . For where your treasure is, there your heart will be also" (Matt. 6:19–21). Earthly pursuits often leave us feeling empty or unfulfilled. But when the Lord is our primary source of happiness then no other disappointment can steal our joy from us. Not even when the deer eat our marigolds. By the way, next year I'm getting geraniums.

If that is how God clothes the grass of the field, which is here today and tomorrow is thrown into the fire, will he not much more clothe you, O you of little faith? (Matt. 6:30)

The first real successes I had at gardening were annuals. I bought several six-packs of impatiens and marigolds, transplanted them into big pots on the front steps, and had an entire summer of lovely flowers adorning our new home. What could be easier? The next year I had equal success planting zinnia and cosmos seeds, both of which are also annuals, in the backyard. They eventually grew to produce a dazzling display of flowers that continued to blossom throughout the summer. Then, they were gone. Annuals are flowering plants that complete their life cycle in one year. Unlike perennials that flower for a short period but return every year, annuals remain in bloom for a good part of their single season. Professional growers continually seek ways to produce annuals that are more colorful and longer growing. When these plants reach full bloom, it is as if they have poured their entire life into one grand performance. God created these flowers for that one burst of glory and they do it . . . gloriously. Their existence, though short, gives testimony to the handiwork of their maker.

In fact, the Scriptures describe the great care He took in designing these short-lived beauties saying, "See how the lilies of the field grow. They do not labor or spin. Yet I tell you that not even Solomon in all his splendor was dressed like one of these" (Matt. 6:28–29). This passage goes on, however, to explain what such concern for mere flowers means to us. If God would put that much thought into creating a plant that will bloom only once, just imagine how much more He cares for us. But we don't have to imagine. He told us himself, urging us to "Cast all your anxiety on him because he cares for you" (1 Pet. 5:7). You might say God cared enough to send flowers. He knew when He created them that their beauty would bring us delight. He also wants us to know that He made them to communicate to us His message of love.

Good Soil

Still other seed fell on good soil, where it produced a crop — a hundred, sixty or thirty times what was sown (Matt. 13:8).

After several years of having snowplows shovel stones from the driveway onto the lawn, the line between the two had vanished. The lawn had receded several feet back, giving way to the advancement of the gravel. Wanting to reclaim the lost ground and restore the original line I went out one spring and thickly covered the area with grass seed. My first attempt, however, ended in utter defeat. First, there were the birds. Hoards of starlings immediately began to devour the new seeds. The survivors that began to grow did so just in time for a dry spell. I tried my best to keep the small shoots alive but soon realized most of the topsoil had been shoveled away so the roots of the new plants had nowhere to grow. The weeds, on the other hand, responded quite well to my watering and soon crowded out the last of the new grass. I finally surrendered and decided to try again in the fall. This time I laid down several bags of topsoil and carefully raked the seeds into the dirt. I ended up with a thick and lovely lawn just in time for the first snow.

My experience with the grass seed was like reliving the parable of the sower and the seed. Jesus used this illustration to describe the hearts of individuals as they heard the Word of God for the first time. Some immediately rejected it and, like the seeds gobbled up by birds, never took root. Others heard and even showed a passing interest but like the plants that never got deeply rooted, they either fell away or remained stunted in their spiritual growth. However, when God's Word was presented to a ready heart we are told, "The one who received the seed that fell on good soil is the man who hears the word and understands it. He produces a crop, yielding a hundred, sixty or thirty times what was sown" (Matt. 13:23). Wow! I bet that kind of faith would even make it through the winter.

The Root of the Problem

Where then did the weeds come from?
(Matt. 13:27).

No matter how bad the drought, I can always count on weeds popping up in our stone driveway. It had reached the point one day where I had to do something. I went out and began furiously pulling them up, one nasty little weed at a time. After an hour (and only a few feet down the driveway) my husband came out suggested that weed killer would do the job completely and effortlessly. He even volunteered to go buy some. But my stubborn streak drove me on until the last weed was pulled. Several hours later, dirty and exhausted, I declared victory. Not a single weed could be seen. Unfortunately, my victory was short-lived. A week later, they were all back. This time, I took my husband up on his offer on the weed killer. While the driveway may have looked completely weed-free, just below the surface the roots had remained untouched. The weed spray took a little longer to work, but the results lasted the rest of the summer because it quite literally got to the root of the problem. It killed the weeds.

Sometimes I approach my spiritual life the same way I tackled the driveway. I tackle my faults by attempting to rid myself of them by sheer willpower. Unfortunately, like weeds, they spring right back up because I haven't gotten to the root of the problem. I was working on "the outward appearance, but the LORD looks at the heart" (1 Sam. 16:7). God knows how to deal with roots and has offered us a permanent one-time weed killer. We are told, "Christ died for sins once for all, the righteous for the unrighteous, to bring you to God" (1 Pet. 3:18). In Jesus, "There is now no condemnation . . . because through Christ Jesus the law of the Spirit of life set me free from the law of sin and death" (Rom. 8:1–2). We can either keep trying to weed out those imperfections and flaws — SINS — in our own strength or we can apply the weed killer once and for all.

To Pull or Not to Pull

Let both grow together until the harvest. At that time I will tell the harvesters: First collect the weeds and tie them in bundles to be burned; then gather the wheat and bring it into my barn (Matt. 13:30).

It was fun getting 32 packages of flower seeds for Christmas. It was fun spending the next few months planning my garden and creating layouts for the seeds. It was even fun planting all 32 packages in the spring. However, it was no longer fun when they all started growing at the same time. Not only was I unable to tell them apart, but I couldn't tell them from the weeds. As everything continued to grow I realized I had no idea what to pull and what not to pull. I discovered too late that I had pulled up every last coneflower while the weeds continued to thrive. Finally, in utter frustration I pulled everything up and started from scratch, this time using already started plants.

I found some comfort in knowing I wasn't the only person to have had this dilemma. It was apparently common enough for Jesus to use as an illustration in one of His parables. He described a man who planted wheat seeds in his field but when they began to grow they were completely inter-mingled with weeds. However, he advised his servants not to pull up the weeds because the wheat would be uprooted along with them. He chose, instead, to wait until harvest and separate them then. Jesus explained the parable saying, "The one who sowed the good seed is the Son of Man. The field is the world, and the good seed stands for the sons of the kingdom. The weeds are the sons of the evil one. . . . As the weeds are pulled up and burned in the fire, so it will be at the end of the age" (Matt. 13:37–40). People sometimes ask why a good God allows evil to go unpunished. He doesn't. While I gave up on my entire garden, flowers and all, God wants no one to perish. The weeds will one day be pulled up but not until all the good seed is ready for His kingdom.

Therefore go and make disciples of all nations, baptizing them in the name of the Father and of the Son and of the Holy Spirit (Matt. 28:19).

I used to love pumpkin pie! A big piece of that custardy pumpkin filling poured into a flaky crust and then just lathered in whipped cream was the perfect end to any meal. Then I was informed that there is no such thing as a pumpkin. Well, at least not botanically speaking. Pumpkins are actually just another variety of squash which, through local traditions, have come to be known as pumpkins. Squash, along with melons and gourds, are all members of the Cucurbitaceae family. The squash most commonly associated with pumpkins are the four species of the genus Cucurbita: C. pepo, C. maxima, C. mixta, and C. moschata. So, there you have it. You won't find pumpkins in the botanical dictionary so there must be no such things as pumpkins. "Of course there are," you say. "I've seen them, touched them, and tasted them!" Relax! Pumpkins are, indeed, in the botanical books. They simply go by another name. A pumpkin by any other name is, at least in my book, still a pumpkin.

There is a word we Christians often use that does not appear in the Bible. Nevertheless, what that word is referring to is not only found in the Scriptures but permeates them. We speak of God the Father, God the Son, and God the Holy Spirit, knowing that all three persons are our one and only God Almighty. The word we use to describe this unique triune oneness He has is the Trinity. Those of us who know Him personally can attest to the existence of each of these distinct persons from our own experience with Him at work in our lives. We pray to our Heavenly Father as we worship His resurrected Son, Jesus Christ. We feel the presence of the Holy Spirit living in our heart and interceding on our behalf to the Father as we pray. Yes, the inarguable proof of the Trinity is both biblical and tangible. Oh, and by the way, I still enjoy eating pumpkin pie!

The Legend of the Trillium

The Son of Man is going to be betrayed into the hands of men. They will kill him, and after three days he will rise (Mark 9:31).

A friend gave me a necklace with a trillium on it as a special thank-you gift. The trillium is a flowering perennial herb of the lily family and, as its name indicates, its flower has three petals. When I expressed my delight at the gift she asked if I'd ever heard the legend of the trillium. The necklace was lovely but the story was even better. As the legend goes, almost 400 years ago a missionary came to tell the Indians about God. When he arrived, he found the particular group of Indians he encountered didn't understand a word of the language he had learned to communicate with them. Desperate to be able to tell them of God's love for them he sought another way to get his message across. One day he noticed some pretty white flowers growing in the forest. They had four petals, which formed the shape of a cross. He used these flowers to explain the crucifixion of Christ to the Indians. Though he was able to make them understand that Jesus died for them, the Indians were merely saddened by the story and began to avoid him.

Realizing what was happening, the missionary then plucked one of the petals from the flower and used the remaining three to describe the concept of the Trinity made up of God the Father, God the Son, and God the Holy Spirit. The little star-shaped green leaves behind the flower also helped him to explain the miracle of Jesus' birth. While the illustration proved to be a great success the missionary was not finished yet. He prayed to the Lord and asked that He would send some sign to remind the Indians of his teachings. God's answer was miraculous. When the little flowers bloomed the following spring they had only three petals, and have remained the same ever since. The story of the trillium is, of course, only a legend. The message of God's love for mankind as demonstrated by His death and resurrection is not only miraculous, it's a fact.

Now learn this lesson from the fig tree: As soon as its twigs get tender and its leaves come out, you know that summer is near (Mark 13:28).

Fig Newtons are the closest I've ever come to seeing a fig tree. It is a low deciduous tree from 15–25 feet tall that only grows in hot, dry climates and produces a crop of soft juicy fruit two or three times per year. The fig tree was, however, quite common in the area where Jesus lived, which made it quite handy when He needed it for an illustration. One day His disciples asked Him about the end of the world saying, "When will these things happen? And what will be the sign that they are all about to be fulfilled?" (Mark 13:4). He began to describe various events that would take place in the last days. There would be wars, natural disasters, persecution of believers, and a world in chaos. After that, He told them, "Men will see the Son of Man coming in clouds with great power and glory" (Mark 13:26). Jesus then pointed to a fig tree and told His disciples that whenever it begins to grow new leaves, you know summer is near. "Even so, when you see these things happening, you know that it is near, right at the door" (Mark 13:29).

Ever since He spoke those words, believers have held on to the lesson of the fig tree as we await our Lord's return. When He gave the illustration, however, Jesus also cautioned against two extremes. First, we are not to try to guess the date. He said, "No one knows about that day or hour, not even the angels in heaven, nor the Son, but only the Father. Be on guard! Be alert! You do not know when that time will come" (Mark 13:32–33). We are also not to give up but to continually "Be on guard! Be alert!" So, don't lose hope, believer. We cannot know the exact day He will appear, but we do know that day is coming soon. As sure as the fig tree blossoms in the summer, our Lord will come to gather His children. Think about that the next time you eat a Fig Newton.

A Matter of Perspective

After this, Jesus went out and saw a tax collector by the name of Levi sitting at his tax booth. "Follow me," Jesus said to him (Luke 5:27).

When I was young I loved them. I would pick them by the armful and weave them together into dandelion chains to wear as necklaces. At some point things changed and the dandelions I once saw as lovely flowers became nothing more than weeds ruining the lawn. While looking up solutions for my dandelion problem I discovered they weren't necessarily the nuisance plants I thought them to be. The dandelion is a stemless perennial or biennial herb of the Compositae flower family. It has long taproots and bright yellow flowers on hollow, stemlike stalks, and far from being a mere weed, it has many practical uses. Its roots contain a substance used as a laxative, and is also roasted and ground as a substitute for coffee. The leaves can be eaten as salad greens, and the flowers are sometimes used for making wine. In Europe the dandelion is even cultivated for some of these useful features. I guess it is all a matter of perspective.

Some look at dandelions and see weeds while others see potential.

When God looks at each of us He sees everything — good and bad, every strength and every flaw. Yet, despite all our weaknesses, He also sees potential. When most people saw nothing but a detestable tax collector, Jesus looked at Levi and saw a faithful disciple. What others saw as a prostitute, Jesus saw as a precious soul in need of grace, which is how He sees each of us. He understands that "All have turned away, they have together become worthless; there is no one who does good, not even one" (Rom. 3:12). Dandelions can be seen as worthless weeds or as valuable herbs. It's all a matter of perspective. From God's perspective we were of enough value to die for. We read, "But we see Jesus . . . now crowned with glory and honor because he suffered death, so that by the grace of God he might taste death for everyone" (Heb. 2:9). In all who believe this, God not only sees potential, He sees Jesus. What could be more lovely!

Good Things to Come

This is the one about whom it is written: "I will send my messenger ahead of you, who will prepare your way before you" (Luke 7:27).

They aren't the most impressive flowers one can grow, but they are, nevertheless, among the most popular. After a long, cold winter there is nothing more delightful than to see the first crocuses of the new year popping out of the ground. The tiny bulbs are planted in the fall just before the first frost. Then, early the next spring these little bearers of good news burst out of the frozen and sometimes snow-covered earth bringing color to the otherwise gray and dreary scenery. Perhaps even more than their physical beauty, it is what they represent that make so many of us plant crocuses all over our yards. Their early arrival is a sign of spring, bringing the hope of a new season full of color and life.

Not too long ago, mankind was living in a wintry darkness. We were spiritually lost and without hope but there, in our darkness, the promise came. A Savior was coming and we were told to look for a sign in anticipation of His arrival. There would be "A voice of one calling: 'In the desert prepare the way for the LORD; make straight in the wilderness a highway for our God' " (Isa. 40:3) and then "the glory of the LORD will be revealed" (Isa. 40:5). As promised, John the Baptist preached those very words, and shortly after, Jesus arrived and accomplished His plan of salvation. Today, much of the world remains in spiritual darkness, but once again we wait for the fulfillment of His promise and the sign we are to look for: "At that time the sign of the Son of Man will appear . . . coming on the clouds of the sky, with power and great glory. . . . will gather his elect . . . from one end of the heavens to the other" (Matt. 24:30-31). Crocuses are a colorful sign of the arrival of spring. The hope of a new season, however, can't compare to all that awaits those who are eagerly looking for the sign of the Son's arrival.

The Son of Man must suffer many things . . . and he must be killed and on the third day be raised to life (Luke 9:22).

Ever wonder how they get those Easter lilies to bloom just in time for the holiday? There is actually quite a science to the whole process. Accurate timetables must be followed for every stage of growth so that the professional growers can count on blooms that will open on schedule. First, the bulbs are precooled for a minimum of four weeks. Then they are planted in small pots and kept in progressively warmer temperatures, and brighter light conditions until they form flower buds. Once the plants are blooming, they are often moved back to a colder area to slow their growth and keep the flowers fresh right up until the Easter lily sales begin. Hence, the process of raising the beautiful white lilies we so enjoy at Easter is a matter of perfect timing.

The Easter holiday is the celebration of another kind of raising. We celebrate Jesus having risen from the grave, which was an event that proved to be of miraculously perfect timing. First, it was the perfect time in human history for Jesus to appear on earth. All of the prophecies of His coming pointed to this time and place, and His death and resurrection perfectly fulfilled each one down to the last detail. It was also the perfect time in the calendar year for His death and resurrection. Jesus was crucified precisely at the time of the Jewish Passover, which fulfilled the messianic prophecies found in the Passover ceremony of the sacrificial lamb who would take away the sins of the world. His body remained in the grave throughout the Jewish Sabbath or day of rest. Then, like white lilies opening on Easter Day, He rose, perfect and sinless, from the grave, bringing forgiveness of sins and the hope of eternal life to mankind. So enjoy your lilies this Easter knowing all the work that went into their perfectly timed blooms. Then, remember the work that Jesus did on the cross so that we, too, can be whiter than snow.

If that is how God clothes the grass of the field, which is here today, and tomorrow is thrown into the fire, how much more will he clothe you, O you of little faith! (Luke 12:28).

Never have I seen a flower more appropriately named than the day lily. One day there is nothing but green stalks, and literally the next day, an explosion of flowers. However, wait just one more day and they are gone. The day lily or *Hemerocallis* is a showy garden perennial of the lily family. It forms loosely clustered, multi-colored flowers on tall stalks that, as its name suggests, last only a day. Fortunately, since each plant has multiple flowers, the blooms of the individual flowers are staggered so it has an extended period of color. Jesus must have been referring to the day lily when He told His disciples to consider the lilies. He said that though they last no longer than a day, God clothed them more colorfully than a king. Surely, if He cared that much about day lilies, we can trust Him to provide for all our needs.

There is another place in the Bible that describes flowers that are here today and gone tomorrow. Here, however, they are used to remind us of the brevity of our own lives. We read, "All men are like grass, and all their glory is like the flowers of the field; the grass withers and the flowers fall" (1 Pet. 1:24). That's the bad news. But the point of the illustration was to contrast our physical bodies with what awaits God's people. He tells us, "For you have been born again, not of perishable seed, but of imperishable, through the living and enduring word of God . . . the word of the Lord stands forever" (1 Pet. 1:23–25). It is interesting to note that while day lilies last only a day, their counterparts, the white lilies, last much longer. White lilies, also known as Easter lilies, are symbolic of purity and of the Resurrection. When compared to day lilies, the Easter lily paints the picture of us leaving our earthly, mortal bodies to receive our new, resurrected bodies. We will be here today, home for eternity.

Then he told this parable: "A man had a fig tree, planted in his vineyard, and he went to look for fruit on it, but did not find any" (Luke 13:6).

It was a perfectly healthy-looking hydrangea plant covered with new growth. It had just one problem; it never flowered. I had carefully followed the planting instructions the previous fall, which assured me that if I did everything correctly, I would have flowers the following summer. For some reason, unknown to me, it didn't happen. My gardening book offered several explanations as to why plants don't flower. One of the more common reasons is plant immaturity. Some plants must reach a certain age before they begin to flower. Another factor is the growing conditions, such as the amount of sunlight or coldness of the winter, may not be suitable enough to allow flowering. Improper pruning is another common reason plants fail to flower. Some bloom only on the previous year's wood so cutting them back improperly can remove all the flowering wood. Hydrangeas in particular carry flower buds at the branch tips through the winter and are often pruned off in the spring. I now knew why I had no hydrangeas.

The Scriptures tell us that Christians can be recognized by their fruit (Matt. 7:20). However, we sometimes fail to produce any fruit at all for reasons similar to those of flowering plants. First, immaturity is a common cause for fruitlessness in the lives of believers. It is essential that we are growing in our faith if we want to have productive lives. This brings us to the importance of the right growing conditions. We will not mature if we don't have enough of the ingredients essential to growth. We need ample exposure to the light through time spent in the Bible, in prayer, and with fellow believers. Pruning is done as we allow the Lord to work in our lives and are responsive to His leading. If we continually make choices that go against His will, we are pruning off the buds that eventually bear flowers. Want to be known by your fruit? Just hand the pruning sheers back to Him and get growing!

Six Little Tomatoes

Or suppose a woman has ten silver coins and loses one . . . when she finds it, she calls her friends and neighbors together and says, "Rejoice with me; I have found my lost coin" (Luke 15:8–9).

There was a small, sunny space in the back yard that was beckoning me to plant something in it. I found a great sale on a six-pack of tomato plants and planted them that very night even though it was still early in the planting season. Since the weather forecast was predicting a cool week I went out each night and covered my six little tomato plants with plastic. One morning I went out to remove the plastic and discovered, to my great surprise, only five little tomato plants. I looked carefully at the spot where the sixth plant had been the night before and saw no sign of anything having even been there. The plant was simply gone. I spent that evening driving around town trying to buy one little tomato plant to replace the one I had lost but no one was selling single plants. Finally, after several days I found a garden shop that sold individual potted tomato plants. I victoriously went home and restored my row of six little tomato plants.

I don't know what the first little tomato plant fell prey to. I do know that for some reason it was very important for me to replace it. My long and frustrating search reminded me of two stories Jesus told about individuals who had lost something important to them. First, He described a man who owned 100 sheep. When one ran away, the man left the other 99 and searched the countryside until he found his lost sheep. Then, He told of a woman who had 10 coins. When one got lost she, too, searched diligently until the missing coin had been found. Then Jesus got to the point saying, "In the same way, I tell you, there is rejoicing in the presence of the angels of God over one sinner who repents" (Luke 15:10). Every single person is important to God. He longs for every lost soul to be restored to a faith in Him and when one does, even the angels rejoice.

If anyone is thirsty, let him come to me and drink. Whoever believes in me, as the Scripture has said, streams of living water will flow from within him (John 7:37–38).

If you happen to have a boggy or damp area you'd like to do something with, you might consider a water garden. The use of water gardens dates from as far back as 2000 B.C. They vary greatly in style depending on location, climate, culture, and personal taste. Your water garden can be virtually anything you want it to be. Formal water gardens are usually made with rectangular or circular pools and contain one or two water lilies and a fountain. Informal water gardens are made with an irregular or natural-shaped pool and generally contain a profusion of different plants suited to a watery environment. Water lilies are the plants most commonly used since they do well in still water that is several feet deep. Japanese water gardens are another popular style and include such additions as ornamental lanterns of stone, or a flat trellis extending over the water. The only condition necessary to creating a successful water garden (other than having the water itself) is to be sure you include suitable oxygenating plants to keep the water clear and support any fish or turtles you decide to add.

Despite the many different forms they come in, all water gardens have one vital feature in common — water. The Church shares this same characteristic with water gardens. The various members of God's church come in all different shapes and sizes. Its individual assemblies represent every imaginable culture and style of worship. But we all have one vital feature in common — living water. Speaking of himself, Jesus said, "If you knew the gift of God and who it is that asks you for a drink, you would have asked him and he would have given you living water" (John 4:10). Jesus is the living water and in Him lies "a spring of water welling up to eternal life" (John 4:14). And all of us who believe in Him, differences and all, are part of His living water garden.

Jesus said to her, "I am the resurrection and the life.
He who believes in me will live, even though he dies"
(John 11:25).

It's hard to believe that anyone would select
something based on how it dies. Yet, that is the
very feature of the maple tree that makes it such
a favorite among gardeners. Catalogs describe
the different varieties in terms of their fall colors.
The sugar maple is recognized by its fiery hues of
orange and gold, the red maple for its spectacular reds and yellows, and the October glory for its
green foliage that turns to crimson red. Maple
trees are deciduous, which means that their leaves
shed or fall off at the end of the season. Their
dramatic colors are short-lived or temporary.
Those lovely colors are actually caused by the
leaves dying. They eventually fall to the ground
leaving the tree bare, but not to worry! The dead
leaves will soon be replaced by new ones as the
life of the tree comes full circle. While it is always
sad to see the last of the leaves fall from their
branches, we realize that unless they do, there

will be no place for new ones to come.

The same thing could be said about us humans and our moral, earthly bodies. They must eventually be shed if we are to put on new ones. The Bible explains, "There are also heavenly bodies and there are earthly bodies; but the splendor of the heavenly bodies is one kind, and the splendor of the earthly bodies is another. . . . So will it be with the resurrection of the dead. The body that is sown is perishable, it is raised imperishable; it is sown in dishonor, it is raised in glory; it is sown in weakness, it is raised in power" (1 Cor. 15:40–43). The fact is, we can't even begin to imagine all we will one day be once this present season passes and we shed the current bodies we are living in. Like the maple tree, we will only start to show our true colors after we have died.

A Single Seed

I tell you the truth, unless a kernel of wheat falls to the ground and dies, it remains only a single seed. But if it dies, it produces many seeds (John 12:24).

Jesus often used parables to describe spiritual concepts in terms the common person could grasp. For three years He taught His disciples, repeatedly using illustrations from the garden to make His point. He told them the story of the sower who planted his seeds in various conditions to describe the different reactions people have to God's word. He used the tiny mustard seed to show what they could accomplish with even the smallest amount of faith. He pointed to the beautifully clothed lilies of the field to remind them of His promise to provide for all their needs. When it came time to explain why He had to die, He once again turned to the garden. He told them that unless a seed falls to the ground and dies "it remains only a single seed. But if it dies, it produces many seeds." Jesus wanted them to understand the necessity of His death. Had He remained there with them He would not have accomplished what He had been sent to do.

He would have remained only a single seed. But through His death, a seed would be planted from which countless new lives would come.

The illustration of the single seed does not end at its death, however, because from death springs life. Jesus wanted His disciples to realize from His death would come His resurrection, springing to the hope of eternal life for all mankind. Jesus said, "I am the resurrection and the life. He who believes in me will live, even though he dies; and whoever lives and believes in me will never die" (John 11:25–26). Like that single seed, Jesus was planted to produce new life, for himself and for all who believe in Him. We are told, "If we have been united with him like this in his death, we will certainly also be united with him in his resurrection" (Rom. 6:5). Countless generations would come from that single seed. If His disciples didn't get it before, they do now.

He cuts off every branch in me that bears no fruit, while every branch that does bear fruit he prunes so that it will be even more fruitful (John 15:2).

Even an amateur gardener knows how important pruning is. In fact, it plays an essential role in the care and maintenance of trees and plants. When done properly, pruning accomplishes several purposes. First, it improves both the appearance and the health of a plant. It also controls the size of a plant. Pruning larger plants and trees can help prevent personal injury or property damage. It is used to train young plants so they will grow stronger or in a particular direction, and it rejuvenates older trees or shrubs causing them to form new growth. Finally, pruning influences flowering and increases fruit production. Wow, all that just from putting a good pair of shears to work!

Perhaps that is why the Bible uses the illustration of pruning to describe how the Lord works in the lives of His children. He wants to accomplish many of the same goals in us. First, He wants to improve our spiritual health, both in our inner spirit and in how our faith is manifested to others. He also wants to see us grow in spiritual depth and understanding. His pruning protects us from personal injury by guiding us away from bad influences and wrong choices. It helps those who are young in their faith to grow stronger, while renewing and reviving those who have been believers for a long time. But above all, He prunes us so that we will be "more fruitful," carefully trimming away the things in our lives that keep us from drawing closer to Him. He explains, "No branch can bear fruit by itself; it must remain in the vine. Neither can you bear fruit unless you remain in me. . . . If a man remains in me and I in him, he will bear much fruit; apart from me you can do nothing" (John 15:4–5). Now pruning may cause us a bit of discomfort, but the end product is well worth the pain. God's intent is "that your joy may be complete" (John 15:11) and He'll be rejoicing with you at harvest time.

Big Tomatoes

This is to my Father's glory, that you bear much fruit (John 15:8).

It was my first attempt at growing tomatoes. I purchased a half-dozen of the healthiest-looking beefsteaks I could find, and tenderly planted the young shoots, using plenty of fertilizer and mulch. I faithfully watered them every day and the little plants quickly shot up to an impressive height. The first signs of fruit appeared as the plants continued to grow. In fact, they were getting to be so tall I was starting to think my tomatoes might break some kind of world record. I was quite surprised when what I actually harvested looked more like cherry tomatoes than beefsteaks. I produced an entire crop of small, pathetic-looking tomatoes. I later discovered that letting the plants grow so tall was where I went wrong. I learned that once the plant has grown four flower bunches one should pinch out the top. That way, the plant can spend its energy producing fruit rather than gaining height. My plants had used all the strength they had in growing so there was nothing left for them to produce fruit. I ended up at a roadside stand for my tomatoes that year.

The Bible urges us to live fruitful lives. Sometimes, however, we put all our energy into our outward appearance, social status, or material possessions. That can leave us with little or no evidence of the fruit God can produce, such as love, goodness, kindness, or joy. To grow spiritual fruit like that we need a good pruning. Jesus said, "I am the true vine, and my Father is the gardener. He cuts off every branch in me that bears no fruit, while every branch that does bear fruit he prunes so that it will be even more fruitful. . . . No branch can bear fruit by itself; it must remain in the vine. . . . If a man remains in me and I in him, he will bear much fruit" (John 15:1-5). Want big tomatoes? Pinch their tops. Want to produce spiritual fruit? Let Jesus do the pinching for you. Then get ready for a feast!

Covered

*My prayer is not that you take them out of the world
but that you protect them from the evil one*
(John 17:15).

As I headed home I realized I had some quick
decisions to make. The weatherman was predicting
the first widespread frost of the season and I had a
yard full of thriving plants to deal with. There
would be no chance of anything surviving the night
but I still had several options. First, I could bring
some plants inside. I brought in the potted flowers
and picked all of the still green tomatoes knowing
they would still ripen indoors. I picked bunches of
flowers and put them in vases all around the house
for a final farewell to summer. There were still a
few small gardens outside that I simply wasn't
ready to part with just yet. Those, I carefully
covered with large sheets of plastic. The frost hit as
expected but the next morning when it had melted
off I went out and removed the coverings and was
able to enjoy my gardens for several more weeks.

When we go through tough times in life,
seasons of frosty trials, we often cry out to God for

His help. While He always hears, and always answers, He too, has several options in how to best respond to our needs. Sometimes He removes us from our difficulties. Like those potted plants and tomatoes I brought into the house, He does not make us face the thing we had prayed for Him to take away. Other times, however, He chooses to allow us to go through the situation we so dreaded, not because He is uncaring but because He cares so much! As His precious children, we will always find that even in the most difficult situations we face we are completely covered by our Heavenly Father's blanket of love. He has promised not only to see us safely through every difficult situation but also to cause it to work out to our benefit. Then, after the trial has passed, we will find we have grown stronger in our faith and deeper in our love for Him.

Those who had been scattered preached the word wherever they went (Acts 8:4).

It was such a great bargain I had no choice but to get it — 50 tulip bulbs for only $2.98! After some careful thought, envisioning the spring season, I planted them in the small garden outside our bedroom window. *How lovely,* I thought, *to wake up one day and see spring blooming in the backyard.* I got all the bulbs in before the first frost then settled in for the long winter's wait. Sure enough, almost nine months later I saw the first signs of tulip petals springing out of the ground. Within weeks the desolate looking yard had burst forth in living color. As we gazed out the window a sea of multicolored tulips greeted us from the garden. All except one. Growing, quite literally, out of the middle of the lawn, was a singular red tulip. *Now how in the world did that get there?* I thought to myself. It became the topic at work the next day. The consensus was that a squirrel must have dug up one of the bulbs and buried it in the middle of the yard.

I looked out at that one lovely tulip brightening up its small spot on the lawn and wondered if my life had that kind of effect on others. It is so easy for us to hang out with our church friends, cloister in our Christian fellowship groups, and never leave the garden. In the days when the New Testament was being written, believers did not have that luxury. People were persecuted for being followers of Jesus. The Bible tells us that churches were constantly being broken up and their members scattered all over the world. History testifies, however, that this did not destroy the Church. On the contrary, the believers shared their faith everywhere they went, adding daily to the number of followers. What was meant to put a stop to the spreading of Christianity only furthered it. That's because, regardless of how they got there, some brave men and women were faithful to bloom where they were planted.

God anointed Jesus of Nazareth with the Holy Spirit and power, and how he went around doing good and healing all who were under the power of the devil (Acts 10:38).

I bought them because they were purple, my favorite color. I had also been told the purple coneflower was an easy-to-grow, self-seeding perennial. Sure enough, this lovely daisy-like flower with its vibrant purple petals livened up my garden the first season I planted it. It was only after I brought a vase of them to work when I learned of the amazing medicinal value many credit this flower with. The purple coneflower, also known as echinacea, is one of the top-selling herbal supplements in America today. It is most commonly used to fight colds and the flu but has also been used to treat such ailments as mastitis, abscesses, cystitis, diverticulitis, hay fever, and wounds. It is said to accomplish all of this by working with the body's own defensive mechanisms to improve its immune system. Echinacea contains polysaccharides called echinacins, which bind to cells and help to prevent pathogens, things that make you sick, from invading the body.

The healing powers of the echinacea sound almost too good to be true. There is a spiritual supplement, however, which is guaranteed to exceed our highest expectations. The Holy Spirit is given to everyone who invites Jesus into his or her life. We are told, "But you will receive power when the Holy Spirit comes on you" (Acts 1:8). Talk about healing power! This is no herb, but God's very presence within us, the "spirit of power, of love and of self-discipline" (2 Tim. 1:7). His Spirit binds to ours and works with our spiritual defensive mechanisms. He prevents our spiritual pathogen, Satan, from invading us so we are no longer controlled "by the sinful nature but by the Spirit" (Rom. 8:9). The dosage? Once for eternity. He has "set me free from the law of sin and death" (Rom. 8:2) and has promised, "Never will I leave you; never will I forsake you" (Heb. 13:5). So step aside, echinacea. Just look at "what Christ has accomplished through me . . . by the power of signs and miracles, through the power of the Spirit" (Rom 15:18–19).

Divided They Grow

Now those who had been scattered by the persecution. . . . The Lord's hand was with them, and a great number of people believed and turned to the Lord (Acts 11:19–21).

You want more plants? Try dividing the ones you have. Most perennials divide quite easily and the procedure is quite simple. The first time I attempted splitting some obedience plants I was a bit hesitant until I read a rather graphic description of what the procedure involves. The planting guide stated, "All you have to do is think like a machete. Hi-yah! One mighty whack and you are done." Now for the gentler souls the instructions recommended thinking more like a comb. It said to "get down on your knees and examine the base of the plant, right at the soil level. Brush the stalks apart and look for a natural dividing line in the plant in the same way you would part your hair in the mirror." When you find a definite point of separation, place your spade on the surface and then prepare to dig. The final advice was clear: "Don't be shy. When bearing such sharpened implements, divide and conquer." Now properly armed for battle, I had great success splitting up my flowers. I also found that the new plants quickly filled in their new space.

God must have had a similar garden building plan in mind with the early church. Becoming a Christian was not a popular thing to do back in New Testament times. On the contrary, some were even martyred for their faith. While He could have protected them and kept them all safely locked away together, God allowed them to face some very severe persecution. Many young churches were forcibly split up and their members scattered. One would think it wouldn't have taken much to squash this movement. One good "Hi-yah" should have put an end to it altogether. But the attacks and persecution had quite the opposite effect. Instead of dying out, God's church only continued to grow because everywhere they went they boldly shared their faith. Like those divided perennials, the believers quickly filled their new space with "the fragrance of the knowledge of him" (2 Cor. 2:14).

Symbiosis

I long to see you . . . that you and I may be mutually encouraged by each other's faith (Rom. 1:12).

I had raved about my mother-in-law's magnificent peony plants and the giant bursts of white and pink flowers they produced each year. I shouldn't have been surprised when she got me a peony plant of my own. She also gave me two instructions. First, she told me not to plant the peony too near the house since peonies attract ants. She then cautioned me *not* to try to remove the ants from the plant. She explained how she had once gone out and sprayed all the ants off of the newly formed buds only to find they never bloomed that year. It seemed that the ants played a necessary part in the blooming process. This kind of relationship where two different species live side-by-side is called "symbiosis." There are several different kinds of symbiotic relationships, but the relationship of the peony with the ants is called mutualism, meaning both partners benefit from the relationship. To state it simply, they need each other.

Our Creator desired a symbiotic relationship with mankind. In fact, that is why He created us — to have a mutually beneficial relationship with us. He also made us to be interdependent with each other. People need each other as much as the peony needs the ants. That is not a weakness, however. It is one of our greatest strengths, because when we work together we can accomplish almost anything. That is why God urged us to "make every effort to do what leads to peace and to mutual edification" (Rom. 14:19). He said, "If you have any encouragement from being united with Christ, if any comfort from his love, if any fellowship with the Spirit, if any tenderness and compassion, then make my joy complete by being like-minded, having the same love, being one in spirit and purpose" (Phil. 2:1–2). Unlike other symbiotic creatures, those of us who have a personal relationship with Him have both the means and the motivation to be united with our fellow believers. When we work together with Him, we can change the world.

And you, though a wild olive shoot, have been grafted in among the others and now share in the nourishing sap from the olive root (Rom. 11:17)

I love lilacs but am always frustrated by the brevity of their flowering season. So, when I read an ad describing the butterfly bush as a lilac-like bush that flowered throughout the summer I was sold immediately. Butterfly bushes come in various shades including lilac, white, and a deep purple. The ad even offered a butterfly bush that could produce flowers in all three colors *on the same bush*. This amazing effect could only be accomplished by grafting. Grafting is the process of joining two or more different plants together to grow as one. There are, of course, certain limitations as to what kind of plants can be successfully grafted together. While there are exceptions, in general only closely related plants can form a compatible union such as apple to apple, rose to rose, or butterfly bush to butterfly bush.

The process of grafting is similar to what happens when a person chooses to become a

Christian. The Lord takes each of us who place our lives into His hands and lovingly grafts us into His family tree. However, unlike trees, there are no limits to the kind of people God can graft into His family. He has taken people with nothing in common, sometimes even former enemies, and has joined them into a perfectly compatible union. The Bible explains, "For he himself is our peace, who has made the two one and has destroyed the barrier, the dividing wall of hostility. . . . His purpose was to create in himself one new man out of the two, thus making peace, and in this one body to reconcile both of them to God through the cross, by which he put to death their hostility" (Eph. 2:14–16). He has grafted each of us, rich and poor, male and female, black and white, into one body — His body. United in Him, our differences become our strength and our diversity makes us the most colorful of all His creations this side of heaven (*and* the other).

Broken Branches

Branches were broken off so that I could be grafted in (Rom. 11:19).

We had a major windstorm a few years ago in which the entire city lost power for several days. That so many electric lines went down was due in part to all the broken tree limbs and branches. The absence of so many of our city's lovely shade trees will be noticed for years to come. Some of the destruction could have been avoided by better pruning habits, since many tree and limb failures are due to unsound branch attachments. A branch is attached to the trunk in one of two ways. Strong connections will show a single rough ridge of bark pushing out at the intersection of the branch and trunk. When the attachment is weak the bark grows, instead, to create a smooth indentation where the branch and trunk meet somewhat like the sleeve of a tight shirt binding under the arm. The inward-folded bark blocks the top of the branch from joining with the trunk and a weak connection is formed right where the branch is subjected to the greatest force during strong winds. The results are split trunks or ripped branches.

The Scriptures compare new believers to branches that have been grafted into a tree. Like those branches, if we are to survive the winds of life it is crucial that we have been properly attached. There are two ways one can be connected to God's family, but only one provides an unbreakable bond, and that is by faith. We are told, "For it is by grace you have been saved, through faith — and this not from yourselves, it is the gift of God — not by works, so that no one can boast" (Eph. 2:8–9). Those who try to join themselves to the Body through their own efforts will only be able to hold until the first real storm hits. Those who have been permanently attached by faith in Him will remain secure through the wildest of tempests because He is the One doing the holding. There won't be any broken branches in that storm.

Of a Different Color

Do not conform any longer to the pattern of this world, but be transformed by the renewing of your mind. Then you will be able to test and approve what God's will is — his good, pleasing and perfect will (Rom. 12:2).

I watched in curiosity as my roommate ran out to the garden with a bottle of lime. She had just bought two identical hydrangea plants and planted them side by side in the garden. Though they had not yet bloomed, the labels on both plants called them blue hydrangeas. "What are you doing?" I asked. "You'll see," she said, but it would be many months before I would discover what she had done. The following summer both hydrangeas blossomed into gigantic flowering balls of color, but to my amazement one was blue and the other was a gorgeously rich shade of pink. My roommate had realized that the soil in our yard was made up of a high alkaline content, which causes hydrangeas to produce blue flowers. By adding lime to the soil around one of the plants she caused the second plant to bloom in pink.

The hydrangea's colors are determined by the kind of soil it is planted in. This is a characteristic we humans have as well. We are all, in many ways, products of our environment. How we dress, the language we speak, and what we become is based largely on our culture and upbringing. There are some areas, however, where being products of our environment is not such a good thing. Peer pressure has caused many people to do and say things they otherwise would not have. Even our faith can be greatly affected by our surroundings and the people we spend time with. But with the right additives to our soil, it does not have to be. We are told, "It is God who works in you to will and to act according to his good purpose . . . so that you may become blameless and pure, children of God without fault in a crooked and depraved generation, in which you shine like stars in the universe" (Phil. 2:13-15). Add God to the equation by inviting Him into our hearts and nothing can stop us from showing our true colors.

I consider that our present sufferings are not worth comparing with the glory that will be revealed in us (Rom. 8:18).

Some seeds need a little extra help to grow. Or, as one gardening magazine put it, they need a little "nick in the pants." Scarification is a technique that is used to speed up the growing process in certain seeds. The word "scarification" means "to scar or nick" and this is quite literally what is done to the seed coat to enhance germination. In natural conditions this coat would eventually be broken down by itself but the gardener can speed the process by using a knife or file to make a shallow cut. This allows moisture to enter and the seed to germinate. For many seeds, merely immersing them in water will do the job. Others need only to be exposed to a certain amount of sunlight. However, larger, hard seeds such as those of the moonflower will rarely germinate unless their coat has been scarified.

There are times when we, too, need a little nick in the pants for a loving God to get our attention. Our doubts, fears, or past hurts can cause us to raise barriers between Him and us that we cannot break down on our own. Like the moonflower, more drastic measures need to be taken if we are to be freed from our hardened shell. Sometimes the Lord will, therefore, allow difficulties and trials into our lives to draw us back to His loving arms. Knowing that, we can "greatly rejoice, though now for a little while you may have had to suffer grief in all kinds of trials. These have come so that your faith — of greater worth than gold . . . may be proved genuine and may result in praise, glory and honor when Jesus Christ is revealed" (1 Pet. 1:6–7). If God chooses to scarify us it will be well worth any momentary discomfort we experience. When we finally open our heart up to Him, He will fill it with a love that bursts forth in living color. Our temporary pain will be completely forgotten in the joy of being reunited with Him.

And again, Isaiah says, "The Root of Jesse will spring up, one who will arise to rule over the nations; the Gentiles will hope in him" (Rom. 15:12).

I read about an interesting elementary school experiment that shows kids how roots function. A carrot with its tip cut off is placed in a glass of red-colored water. After several days the carrot is removed from the water and split open lengthwise. Throughout the carrot red lines indicate where the water was taken up by the plant. The carrot itself is a taproot. A taproot is more than just a big root growing below a plant. It is the main root. It is actually an extension of the main stem growing straight down into the ground. From this central root numerous smaller roots grow. Many perennials, bushes, and almost all trees have a taproot. If the tip of the taproot is cut off in transplanting a tree, if it survives at all, it will be stunted instead of growing tall and straight. The taproot is critical to the life of the plant because it conducts the water it needs from the soil. It also keeps the plant held securely in place even in strong winds.

The Bible describes Jesus as the Root of Jesse. Isaiah had prophesied His coming saying, "In that day the Root of Jesse will stand as a banner for the peoples; the nations will rally to him, and his place of rest will be glorious" (Isa. 11:10). He said He would be "like a root out of dry ground" (Isa. 53:2). The apostle Paul quoted Isaiah's prophecies to the believers at Rome. The Root had, indeed, sprung up during their own lifetime but then He was gone. Had the taproot been cut off? Would the entire tree of believers perish? No, as both Isaiah and Paul explained, He is a risen Lord, a thriving Root. We are told, "Do not weep! See, the Lion of the tribe of Judah, the Root of David, has triumphed" (Rev. 5:5). A plant is only as strong as its taproot. We will be held securely and eternally in place by the Root of Jesse.

Follow my example, as I follow the example of Christ (1 Cor. 11:1).

I owe my love for gardening to my mom. I remember when she bought me my first gardening kit. She knew that if she was going to spark any interest in me it would need to be something easy to plant and successful to grow. What she decided upon accomplished both objectives and, even better, it was purple! Mom knew I love purple and she found a kit called the complete purple garden. If I had any doubts about gardening they were quickly dispelled when I saw that. According to the instructions, one needed only to plant the various packets of seeds using the suggested layout, and a garden of purple flowers would bloom throughout the summer. For the first time in my life I was motivated to give it a try and my purple garden was such a success I've been gardening ever since.

My mom must have looked long and hard to find a gift so perfectly suited for me. It also showed how well she knows me and how much she loves me. However, the gift itself was not the main reason I came to love gardening. My mom's own example was what ultimately won out. I grew up watching her happily working in the garden, creating exquisite floral displays. I saw the satisfaction it gave her and it made me want to experience that joy for myself. It also taught me a lesson in sharing my faith with others. My mom loved me enough to want to me to experience the pleasure she had found in gardening. Do I care enough about others to want to share the love I have found in God with them? Mom motivated me, primarily, by her own example. Is my relationship with the Lord something that would inspire others to want it for themselves? I enjoy gardening and highly recommend it. I love the Lord with all my heart and there is nothing I could recommend more than for others to experience this love for themselves.

The Merger

I have planted, Apollos watered; but God gave the increase (1 Cor. 3:6;KJV).

In 1995 the two biggest gardening companies in the world merged. It all started back in 1868 when Orlando McLean Scott purchased a hardware store and seed business. That business eventually became the Scott's Company, one of the largest horticulture products companies in the world. In 1950, Otto Stern, a nurseryman and mail order business owner, with the help of an advertising executive, invested $2,000 to introduce a new product to the gardening world. He ran a full-page ad in a New York City newspaper telling people about Miracle-Gro. Three days later $22,000 in mail orders were received, bringing the company almost overnight success. After the two companies merged they established a new headquarters in Ohio and now have facilities and sales organizations all over the world. Two individuals with common visions went from being two small one-man businesses to being the single world leader in lawn and garden products.

There was a similar merger in the beginning days of the Church. The apostle Paul began his solo ministry after a personal encounter with the Lord. Meanwhile, hundreds of miles away, another man named Apollos was also sharing his faith with others. Both men had their own following. They could have become competitors and, in fact, in some of their followers' eyes, they were. But Paul had a greater vision than in taking followers away from Apollos. As he wrote, "Who then is Paul, and who is Apollos, but ministers by whom ye believed. . . . So neither he who plants nor he who waters is anything, but only God, who makes things grow" (1 Cor. 3:5–7). Both men had the same goal, and that was to see new believers come to their Lord and grow in their faith. Both men realized that only God could cause that to happen. These two individuals shared a common vision — that of pointing others to their Savior. That was almost 2,000 years ago and the Church they helped begin has not only reached around the globe but is headed for eternity.

So neither he who plants nor he who waters is anything, but only God, who makes things grow
(1 Cor. 3:7).

Our new house came with an old, dead tree stump in the middle of the front lawn. Rather than dealing with having it removed, I decided to decorate it by planting morning glory seeds around its base. I began to go out every evening with my watering can and walk once around the stump watering the seeds. At one point I noticed the old man sitting on his porch across the street watching me. I smiled and waved but he sat motionlessly and scowled. For the next few weeks he was out there silently glaring at me every time I went out to water. Finally, one day as I was about halfway around the stump, watering can in hand, he leapt to his feet and yelled, "Hey! It ain't gonna grow, you know!" It is no wonder the man had been scowling, thinking he had a new neighbor who was trying to grow a stump. I assured him that was not the case and we both had a good laugh.

It is easy to see the futility of watering a tree

stump. What isn't quite as obvious, but equally futile, is our attempt at making ourselves worthy of God's favor. Trying to be good enough, or work hard enough to please God is like trying to nurture a dead tree. It simply ain't gonna grow. The good news is that God's plan is much easier. He doesn't expect us to take our old sinful nature and make it better. He wants to grow a whole new nature in us. Because of His great love for us, He has given each of us a seed of faith. Those of us who choose to plant our faith in Him will see that new nature begin to blossom. As God's spirit grows within us, His divine nature will replace ours and others will see His loveliness through us. My morning glories eventually bloomed and completely covered the old, dead stump with beautiful flowers. Why, even my neighbor thought it was lovely.

To the weak I became weak, to win the weak. I have become all things to all men so that by all possible means I might save some (1 Cor. 9:22).

You can plant almost anything you want, almost anywhere you want, with a little extra effort and creativity. Still, for the best results and the least effort one should make every attempt to work *with* the natural environment rather than *against* it. Or, as one gardening column I read put it, "Don't try to fight nature." The article explained that while some measures can be taken to make your garden a more hospitable place for particular plants, your experience will be much more rewarding if you learn to work with nature. For example, you can put a plant that requires full sun in a shady spot but it will take more fertilizer and probably produce less impressive flowers than if it was in the full sun. It is always best to learn to work with nature.

Those of us who desire to share our faith in God with others could take a few pointers from this gardening advice. While the message we want to share is an unchanging, uncompromising truth, the way we communicate it can and should be customized to the one we are sharing it with. The intellectual, for example, might be attracted by the historical, archeological, and scientific accuracy of the Scriptures. Someone who is starving, on the other hand, would be much more likely to consider the message of the Bible after receiving a hot meal. Someone who is struggling with loneliness or has suffered a loss might find comfort in the promises of God found in the Word. Another might be most touched by your own personal testimony and what the Lord means to you. Ultimately, it is God, and God alone, who draws people to himself. But if we learn to work with the environment rather than against it, the seeds we plant in the lives of others will have a much better chance of taking root. We can help make the soil those seeds are planted in a much more hospitable place. Then the rest is up to God.

The Hardiness Factor

And God is faithful; he will not let you be tempted beyond what you can bear. But when you are tempted, he will also provide a way out so that you can stand up under it (1 Cor. 10:13).

I had just discovered a new tree I wanted, but before buying it I called a local gardening expert to see if this unique specimen could be grown in our area. The first thing he asked me was what its hardiness zone was. Hardiness zones, also known as growing zones, are a guide to help determine whether plants can manage your region's temperatures. Plants vary in the temperature extremes they can endure. The zones were put together by botanists and horticulturists who gathered weather records throughout North America and compiled a database showing the average coldest temperatures for each region. These records were condensed into a range of temperatures and transformed into various zones of plant hardiness. Maps were then made to show the lines between these temperature zones. The USDA plant hardiness map divides North America into 11 hardiness zones with zone 1 being the coldest and zone 11 being the warmest.

When God transplants us into His family He, too, considers the hardiness factor. We humans also vary in the extremes we can endure. He keeps that in mind when He gives each of us our own unique place in His body. Some will be called to serve Him in foreign lands or to suffer persecution. Others will not. God knows exactly how much each of us can handle and will not push us beyond what we can bear. Nevertheless, He assures us that "Those parts of the body that seem to be weaker are indispensable, and the parts that we think are less honorable we treat with special honor. . . . But God has combined the members of the body and has given greater honor to the parts that lacked it" (1 Cor. 12:22–24). Because God knows our individual strengths and weaknesses we can trust He will not place us in any situation that is outside our hardiness zone. Because He loves us we can rest assured that anything He allows us to go through, we will not only endure but will come through victorious. That's a promise.

On the contrary, those parts of the body that seem to be weaker are indispensable (1 Cor. 12:22).

I was browsing through a gardening catalog in search of new layout ideas. All of the full-color pictures were lovely and each garden had a unique beauty all its own. One in particular stood out as being the most impressive. I pulled out my pencil and started jotting down notes so I could duplicate this exciting look in my own garden. As I began to list the individual flowers I was surprised to find several I would never have thought of using.

Petunias had always struck me as being somewhat commonplace, and I thought of black-eyed Susans as wildflowers. But somehow, in combination with the bright marigolds, purple coneflowers, daylilies, zinnias, and sweet alyssum, the look was stunning. What I had considered uninteresting added ingredients that were essential in creating the magnificent garden pictured before me.

Sometimes we humans are tempted to look at ourselves the way I looked at those black-eyed

Susans. We see ourselves as being less significant than those who have more dynamic personalities or prominent talents. Perhaps we've been bypassed or ignored by those who consider us uninteresting or, even worse, unnecessary. That is not what the Bible says about us. In God's eyes everyone is important. Using the example of a body, He explains how each of His followers is a vital part of it. His Body, "joined and held together by every supporting ligament, grows and builds itself up in love, as each part does its work" (Eph 4:16). We are told that "God has arranged the parts in the body, every one of them, just as he wanted them to be. If they were all one part, where would the body be?" (1 Cor. 12:18–19). Everyone is an essential part of the whole and, in fact, those who seem the least necessary are "indispensable." So, don't pass up those black-eyed Susans for your garden, and don't neglect that special talent the Lord has given you. No matter how insignificant you may think it is, the world won't be quite as beautiful without it.

The Ultimate Recycling Program

What you sow does not come to life unless it dies
(1 Cor. 15:36).

Composting was the topic of our local TV station's nightly gardening tip. It described in detail how to set up a compost pile and what kind of organic materials to add. Even items such as coffee grounds and eggshells could be included in the mix for their great nutrient-adding potential. In about six months a rich new soil is ready for use in the garden. Compost is actually a natural form of recycling, which is continually occurring through decomposition. When a plant dies, its remains are attacked by micro-organisms in the soil. As it decomposes nutrients are recycled in an ecosystem. There are several advantages to composting. Composting greatly reduces public waste disposal. At the same time it proves a nutrient-rich soil. Compost added to gardens improves solid structure, texture, aeration and water retention. It also contributes to erosion control, soil fertility, and healthy root development in plants. Just think! All of this comes from waste materials or, to put it another way, from death springs life.

God designed His world with an amazing ability to naturally recycle itself. As impressive as that is, it is nothing compared to the spiritual recycling business He has. Mankind is its prime recipient and it all begins with our physical death. The Bible explains, "So will it be with the resurrection of the dead. The body that is sown is perishable, it is raised imperishable; it is sown in dishonor, it is raised in glory; it is sown in weakness, it is raised in power; it is sown a natural body, it is raised a spiritual body" (1 Cor. 15:42–44). Unlike the natural world, when God recycles our physical bodies the end product is far superior to the first for "When the perishable has been clothed with the imperishable, and the mortal with immortality, then the saying that is written will come true: 'Death has been swallowed up in victory' " (1 Cor. 15:54). In God's spiritual ecosystem, from death springs not just life, but life eternal.

Fragrances

But thanks be to God, who always leads us in triumphal procession in Christ and through us spreads everywhere the fragrance of the knowledge of him (2 Cor. 2:14).

I was proud of my new butterfly bushes. I had bought them because they were supposed to have lilac-like flowers and attract butterflies, both of which they did quite well. The first year they flowered, these unique bushes also provided an unexpected bonus. I took a bouquet of freshly cut flowers to work one day hoping to dazzle my co-workers with my gardening talents. To add a bit of variety I included a few of the deep purple-colored butterfly bush flowers. From the moment I set the vase on the counter people began commenting on the lovely scent and asked what it was. We all began pulling out flowers one at a time to track down the source of this sweet honey-like fragrance. We soon realized it was the tiny butterfly flowers. By the end of the day those two small branches had filled the entire office with their scent. I discovered it isn't just butterflies that are attracted to the fragrance of the butterfly bush.

God has called each of His children to be an attractive aroma of himself. As we grow in our love for and knowledge of our Savior, we will take the scent of His presence with us wherever we go. As lovely as that butterfly bush fragrance smelled to me, however, there were some who did not like it at all. I even remember it causing one woman with allergies to sneeze. When we bring the fragrance of our Lord to a dying world, it will most assuredly not appeal to everyone. "For we are to God the aroma of Christ among those who are being saved and those who are perishing. To the one we are the smell of death; to the other, the fragrance of life" (2 Cor. 2:15–16). Some will turn up their noses at the scent we wear but when others are drawn to it we will be glad we were willing to share our bouquet of life with the world.

Following the Sun

And we, who with unveiled faces all reflect the Lord's glory, are being transformed into his likeness with ever-increasing glory, which comes from the Lord, who is the Spirit (2 Cor. 3:18).

I had hoped for enough seeds from my row of sunflowers to feed the winter birds. The birds got their seeds, but not quite how I intended. I looked out the window one day to see a pair of large blue jays sitting on top of the flowers helping themselves to the seeds. I enjoyed watching these lovely creatures dining in my garden but had no idea the capacity two birds had. By the next day they had picked every flower clean. The sunflower (of the genus *Helianthus*) is a garden favorite, in part due to its size. It ranges from 3 to 12 feet tall with giant, golden-rayed flower heads up to a foot wide. It is also grown for several practical purposes and is even considered a commercially valuable plant. The flowers yield a yellow dye, and the seeds provide oil and food. The oil is used in soap, paints, and poultry feed. The seeds can be eaten dried or roasted or they can be ground to make bread or a coffee-like beverage. In addition to its sun-like appearance, the sunflower got its name from the way the plant turns its head from east to west to follow the sun.

These giants among flowers can teach us a thing or two. Sunflowers continually follow the sun while at the same time bearing a striking resemblance to it. God has promised that anyone who follows His Son will be named after Him. We will be called the sons of God. As we continue to follow Him, in time, we will also begin to resemble our Heavenly Father. We read, "Dear friends, now we are children of God, and what we will be has not yet been made known. But we know that when he appears, we shall be like him" (1 John 3:2). Sunflowers spend their lives following the sun on its daily course. If we spend our lives following the Son we will one day finish the course and follow Him home.

The Perfect Image

. . . the light of the gospel of the glory of Christ, who is the image of God (2 Cor. 4:4).

I loved it the moment I saw it. My mom had bought several different kinds of small trees to plant around the yard. The little Alberta spruce became an immediate favorite of mine and has been ever since. To me, it was like looking at the perfect image of a giant evergreen tree, only in miniature. The Alberta spruce is a naturally occurring dwarf evergreen tree with a strong conical shape and a formal appearance. It grows very slowly (2 to 4 inches per year) with a maximum height of 4 to 6 feet and rarely needs pruning. Each year it produces lovely bright green needles. This vibrantly colored, dense foliage is what makes the little tree so attractive. Because of its symmetrical, upright shape, bright color, and permanently small size, the Alberta spruce is the perfect container plant or novelty specimen. It also makes a lovely miniature Christmas tree. But what impressed me most about this little tree was that it was the very image of a full-sized evergreen tree. This actually makes perfect sense because it is, in every way, an evergreen tree.

The dwarf Alberta spruce helps illustrate the relationship of Jesus to His Father. While the Bible teaches that Jesus is God, it also clearly illustrates Him as being separate from God the Father. When He came to earth Jesus remained, in every way, fully God, but at that point He had also become fully man. Now remember, mankind was the only creation God made in His own image. Yet most of us would readily agree that because of our sin nature we are far from being a perfect image. Jesus, however, was. In fact, when one of His disciples asked to see His Father, Jesus responded, "Anyone who has seen me has seen the Father" (John 14:9). Because He was both God and a sinless man, He was the only one who could ever truly claim to be the very image of God. And while here, He was that perfect image, in miniature.

Deadheading

Therefore if any man be in Christ, he is a new creature: old things are passed away; behold, all things are become new (2 Cor. 5:17;KJV).

It seemed like only a few days after planting the cosmos seeds that the tiny sprouts first appeared. They quickly continued to grow and in no time at all formed a row of tall and healthy young plants. I was delighted when the multicolored flowers began to bloom just as fast as the plants had grown. Then, only days after they had first appeared, the flowers withered and died. I wondered what people saw in such a short-lived product. A few days later a friend stopped by and informed me that for the best results cosmos needed to be deadheaded. She then showed me how to pinch off each of the flowers that were past bloom. To my amazement, new flowers seemed to appear almost overnight. One small flower was often replaced by two larger ones. As I continued to faithfully deadhead the plants, those cosmos kept flowering all summer long and right through to the fall frosts.

As its name implies, deadheading is the process of removing the old, dead flowers to allow the plant to grow new ones in their place. It is an essential step in producing a beautiful and long-lasting flower garden. It is an equally essential step in one's spiritual growth as well. If we want to see ourselves continue to bloom we need to have some deadheading done in our lives. The Bible urges us to "rid yourselves of all such things as these: anger, rage, malice, slander, and filthy language from your lips. Do not lie to each other, since you have taken off your old self with its practices and have put on the new self, which is being renewed in knowledge in the image of its Creator" (Col. 3:8–10). If we let Him, the Master Gardener will work within us pinching off the old and unsightly nature and replacing it with His very own. With His help we can blossom for the rest of our lives so that even in old age we bring glory to Him in our corner of His garden.

Therefore come out from them and be separate, says the Lord (2 Cor. 6:17).

The mail order company guaranteed that they would ship my order just in time for the fall planting. Unfortunately, they hadn't anticipated the unusually late heat wave that hit the very day the package arrived. However, aware that such events occur, the company also sent a planting guide that told me exactly what to do in this case. Since such unseasonable heat would have caused the bulbs to come out of dormancy prematurely, the instructions said to store them in a cool place such as the refrigerator until they could be safely planted. However, they also warned against storing the bulbs in the same bin with fresh fruit. Ripening fruit produces a gas called ethylene, which will stop bulbs from flowering.

The Bible gives us a similar warning about the kind of company that we keep and the effect it can have on us, saying, "Do not set foot on the path of the wicked or walk in the way of evil men. Avoid it, do not travel on it; turn from it and go on your way" (Prov. 4:14–15). We are cautioned to "watch out for those who cause divisions and put obstacles in your way that are contrary to the teaching you have learned. Keep away from them" (Rom. 16:17). In fact, we are instructed to "avoid every kind of evil" (1 Thess. 5:22). We are also told to "avoid godless chatter, because those who indulge in it will become more and more ungodly" (2 Tim. 2:16).

Eventually, if we continually invest our time in that which is contrary to our beliefs, we will be like bulbs exposed to ethylene. Our lives will remain dormant and ineffective. That is why our loving Heavenly Father urges us, "But you, man of God, flee from all this, and pursue righteousness, godliness, faith, love, endurance and gentleness" (1 Tim. 6:11). If we truly desire to blossom into all God meant us to be we must flee anything that interferes with that goal. Don't lose sight of it. Spring is just around the corner!

And no wonder, for Satan himself masquerades as an angel of light (2 Cor. 11:14).

I wasn't familiar with all the flowers that came in the mixed bulb collection I bought. So I planted the ones I hadn't heard of in a separate area to see whether or not I liked them. One of the new flowers in particular caught my eye. It grew at least a foot taller than the rest and formed a large purple pom-pom-like flower. It was so unique that I included several in a bouquet I took to work. At first my flower arrangement got rave reviews but after a while the comments began to change dramatically. "What's that smell?" I heard people say as they entered the office. Eventually someone yelled out, "Hey, something stinks!" which, at that point, it quite noticeably did. Finally, someone with some gardening experience was able to identify the problem. "Well, no wonder" she declared, "You have onions in your flower arrangement." I learned the hard way that those lovely pom-poms came from allium bulbs, which are members of the onion family.

Alliums are just one example of things in this world that are attractive to the eye but upon closer investigation are actually onions in disguise. Evil often cloaks itself as something lovely and desirable. Satan, the prince of evil himself is referred to as an angel of light who is out to "deceive even the elect — if that were possible" (Matt. 24:24). In the case of my smelly bouquet, all I would have needed to do to spare myself a little embarrassment was to have known what kind of flower I was selecting and to avoid using onions. God has warned us to be alert to the fact that there is an enemy who wants to deceive us. We needn't be afraid, however. "Submit yourselves, then, to God. Resist the devil, and he will flee from you" (James 4:7). When we put our trust in the Lord, Satan will flee even faster than they did from my onion bouquet!

Growing Borders

For he himself is our peace, who has made the two one and has destroyed the barrier, the dividing wall of hostility (Eph. 2:14).

There is an old saying that tall fences make for good neighbors. Right before we moved into our new house the neighbor who lives in back of us (whom we hadn't even met yet) laid a line of railroad ties all the way down the property line between us. What could have been taken as an insult actually ended up helping us out in two ways. First, we knew exactly where our property ended, and second, it gave me the perfect excuse to plant a border garden. Border gardens are a lovely way to turn a dividing line into a festive display of color. I planted all kinds of bulbs, perennials, annuals, and bushes the entire way down the property line, turning the former eyesore into an attraction. Our new neighbor must have liked it, too. He soon came over, introduced himself, and invited me to come over and help myself to some topsoil. Perhaps there is something to that old saying, after all.

Tall fences may help in dealing with neighbors, but in the spiritual realm God is in the business of tearing fences down. While clearly delineated property lines help avoid conflict, in God's kingdom all the property belongs to Him. As His beloved children, we are all co-heirs to His kingdom, but instead of rejoicing together we allow petty differences to come between us. The people who have more in common than anyone else in the world often find themselves separated by these self-imposed fences. God desires all those barriers to be broken down and to see all His children come together in unity. The Scriptures urge us, ". . . in the name of our Lord Jesus Christ, that all of you agree with one another so that there may be no divisions among you and that you may be perfectly united in mind and thought (1 Cor. 1:10). Rather than building walls, we need to work on growing together in Christ. Once the fences are down, we can all get together and enjoy our garden.

Drought Resistance

And I pray that you, being rooted and established in love, may have power, together with all the saints, to grasp how wide and long and high and deep is the love of Christ (Eph. 3:17–18).

It had been an extremely dry season and despite my best attempts at watering, I still lost several young trees before the drought finally ended. Several others, however, came through as healthy and strong as ever. The difference was in how drought resistant each tree was. Drought resistance is the capacity of a plant to withstand periods of dryness. This is achieved through better water uptake from the soil, reduced loss of water, and good water storage. Water from the soil enters the plant through the ends of the roots. The most drought resistant plants have extensive root systems that are capable of rapid growth into deeper soil where more moisture is available. Some trees adapt better to drier areas than others because they have taproots many times longer than the main root system that drill deep into the subsoil for water. Then, even when the surface becomes extremely dry, killing plants with shallower roots, the trees with taproots remain virtually unaffected by the drought.

We are all susceptible to periods of dry spells in our spiritual lives but we can learn a few pointers from the trees on how to better weather those times of spiritual drought. Like the trees that couldn't handle the dry spell, if our faith is superficial, and dependent on circumstances, it may not survive when difficult situations arise. The Scriptures describe such people saying, "Since they have no root, they last only a short time. When trouble or persecution comes because of the word, they quickly fall away" (Mark 4:17). If, however, our faith is deeply rooted in God and His Word we will come through the dry spells unwaveringly. We are told, "So then, just as you received Christ Jesus as Lord, continue to live in him, rooted and built up in him, strengthened in the faith as you were taught, and overflowing with thankfulness" (Col. 2:6–7). If we approach our dry spells this way, we will hardly notice them until they're far behind us.

From him the whole body, joined and held together by every supporting ligament, grows and builds itself up in love, as each part does its work (Eph. 4:16).

When I bought my first lilac bush I was told I would need at least two to produce flowers the first year. I jokingly asked how I could tell if I had picked out a boy and a girl plant. I soon discovered that there was some truth to what I had asked. Plants do, indeed, have male and female parts and they require being pollinated to reproduce. Pollen is a fertilizing body that produces male sperm and is formed in the stamen, or male apparatus, of seed-bearing plants. Through pollination the pollen is transferred to the flower's pistil, or female structure, where it unites with the female egg. The plant is fertilized when a sperm cell in the tube joins the egg cell of the ovule, which then develops into a seed. Some plants have both stamens and pistils and are capable of self-pollination, but most have one or the other and must be fertilized by cross-pollinating with other plants. They rely on external agents, such as bees, hummingbirds, wind, or water to deliver the pollen. The flowers attract these helpers by their color, fragrance, and nectar. Cross-pollination produces sturdier, more adaptable plants. For this reason plant breeders often cross-pollinate plants to produce new varieties.

When the Church functions the way God intended it to, it produces sturdier, more adaptable believers. Like plants, our spiritual growth is greatly enhanced by the external agents, or other believers God brings into our lives. That is why He "gave some to be apostles, some to be prophets, some to be evangelists, and some to be pastors and teachers, to prepare God's people for works of service, so that the body of Christ may be built up" (Eph. 4:11–12). Some believers try to self-pollinate their way to spiritual maturity. But on their own they will never know the joy of being part of a cross-pollinating, mutually encouraging body of believers. Only there can they experience the wonder of spiritual reproduction and, as they share their faith, will see new varieties of believers added to the family.

The Herb Garden

Live a life of love, just as Christ loved us and gave himself up for us as a fragrant offering and sacrifice to God (Eph. 5:1–2).

Herb gardens are one of the latest gardening rages. Gardeners like the challenge of growing a garden that is both practical and attractive. Growing herbs is not new, but dates as far back as biblical times. The Greeks and Romans wrote about herbs and their uses in medicine and cooking. Early physicians used them to treat a variety of ailments. The first American colonists brought herbs with them only to discover even more about the native herbs from the American Indians. Herbs are the aromatic leaves of such plants as parsley, lavender, basil, dill, sage, chive, marjoram, mint, rosemary, and thyme. Most herbs are perennial plants and their main use is in culinary recipes. Though in recent years the medicinal uses of herbs are making a comeback, herbs are still primarily used as seasonings to flavor food. Herbal teas are considered tasty and healthful. Because of their delightfully aromatic nature they are also used in products such as soap, sachets, shampoo, or perfume.

Herbs were important enough to earn their own mention in the creation account. We read, "And God said, Let the earth bring forth grass, the herb yielding seed, and the fruit tree yielding fruit after his kind, whose seed is in itself, upon the earth: and it was so" (Gen. 1:11;KJV). He then explained, "Behold, I have given you every herb bearing seed . . . to you it shall be for meat"(Gen. 1:29;KJV). God created herbs, spices, and seasonings, knowing their pleasing tastes and scents would bring us delight. He also used the example of seasonings to illustrate the role His people would have in bringing the message of our Creator's love to a spiritually hungry world. He has sent us out bearing "the fragrance of the knowledge of him" (2 Cor. 2:14). We all know people don't always like the aroma of a particular herb. Nor will everyone find the scent of our faith attractive. Some, however, will recognize it as the "fragrance of life" (2 Cor. 2:16). So, go ahead. Pour on the seasonings.

Pesticides

Therefore put on the full armor of God, so that when the day of evil comes, you may be able to stand your ground, and after you have done everything, to stand (Eph. 6:13).

Pesticide is an umbrella term for all insecticides, herbicides, fungicides, and rodenticides that are used to kill some living thing. The operative word being "pest," it is a handy tool to use to conquer foes that would otherwise do considerable damage to our gardens. However, there are several precautions that should always be taken before using any pesticide. First, one should consider whether or not the particular application in question is needed. By far the safest means of using pesticides is by not using them at all. If the use of pesticides is warranted, the second basic rule is to always read the entire label fully before starting. Failure to read the directions is one of the main reasons that pesticides are ineffective, and also a main cause of accidental poisoning or damage to others. Remember that pesticides were intentionally designed to be deadly, but when used properly they can literally save our gardens from ruin.

Spiritual warfare should be used in much the same way we approach pesticides. We have a very real and powerful enemy who is out to do as much harm as possible. But God has given us all the pesticides that we need to keep evil away. However, we must be just as careful in reading all the directions or our best attempts at defeating him will be ineffective and could even have adverse affects. The Bible is our instruction manual for dealing with Satan. We are told to put on the full armor God has given us. We must, of course, be sure of our own salvation through faith in Jesus. Then, we should become fully grounded in the truth, in righteousness, and in faith, all of which come through studying and knowing the Scriptures. Prayer is another mighty weapon we've been given. When properly equipped, we can face every spiritual enemy with the assurance that "You, dear children, are from God and have overcome them, because the one who is in you is greater than the one who is in the world" (1 John 4:4).

Container Gardens

Because of my chains, most of the brothers in the Lord have been encouraged to speak the word of God more courageously and fearlessly (Phil. 1:14).

So, you say you don't have enough room in your yard for a garden? Or perhaps you have no yard at all! You might be tempted to think you are not able to have a garden of your own, but by using containers you can have a lovely collection of plants virtually anywhere. In fact, one can even grow a container garden right inside your home. Once one catches the vision, the options are endless as to what can be planted as well as in what it can be planted to create a unique and lovely effect. Containers can be placed on steps, in windows, in the center of a room or on multi-tiered shelves. I have seen plants being grown from buckets, vases, baskets, and even an old toilet bowl (yes, I've really seen someone do this). I once saw someone use an old bed frame to quite appropriately make a "flower bed." My favorite was an old rowboat that someone had turned into a boat garden. One is limited only by one's imagination.

Some people feel that because of the particular situation they are in they can't do anything useful or that their lives won't ever amount to much. So they end up wasting the precious talents and gifts they've been given. Perhaps they need to consider a container garden. What do you feel limits you? For the apostle Paul it was being in prison, but he certainly didn't let that stop him. Right there in his cell he shared his faith, wrote numerous letters which would become a part of the Scriptures, and encouraged all he came in contact with there in his container. So what is it for you? Are you in a wheel chair? A retirement home? A hospital bed? Do you have a speech impediment or physical deformity? If you'll let Him, God would love to help you create a lovely container garden right where you are. Your faith and imagination is your only limit. Just think of the possibilities!

But one thing I do: Forgetting what is behind and straining toward what is ahead, I press on toward the goal to win the prize for which God has called me heavenward in Christ Jesus (Phil. 3:13–14).

When all else fails, try morning glories. Morning glories (also known as *Ipomoea*) are sun-loving plants with bright funnel-shaped blooms that grow on vines. They are quick-growing plants with fragile, short-lived flowers in blue, pink, or purple that need little care and grow in almost any warm climate. They can also be trained to climb and cover virtually any object. I have used them to cover dead stumps and decorate mailbox poles, and have also seen them used to climb trellises, porches, fences, and flagpoles. I have found these tenacious vines can successfully manage to climb their way up virtually any nearby object in their pursuit of the sun. The morning glory derives its name from how the individual flowers close up at night but re-open as soon as the first rays of the morning sun hit them. The entire growing and blooming process of the morning glory revolves around the sun.

Oh, the joy we could experience and the victories we could achieve if we would only revolve our lives around the Son. How He longs for us to "seek him and perhaps reach out for him and find him, though he is not far from each one of us. For in him we live and move and have our being" (Acts 17:27–28). He is our source of life and light. Apart from Him, we are living in darkness. As Isaiah wrote, "The people walking in darkness have seen a great light; on those living in the land of the shadow of death a light has dawned. . . . For to us a child is born, to us a son is given. . . . And he will be called Wonderful Counselor, Mighty God, Everlasting Father, Prince of Peace" (Isa 9:2–6). Since Isaiah wrote these words, the Sonlight has come and shined His Light upon this earth. If we open our hearts to Him and head toward that light, like the morning glories, we will find ourselves effortlessly overcoming every obstacle we face as we climb toward the Son.

Miracle Grow

The whole body, supported and held together by its
ligaments and sinews, grows as God causes it to grow
(Col. 2:19).

"Have you tried Miracle-Gro?" was the first
thing everyone asked when I told them about my
struggling transplanted bushes. I got the same
suggestion when I asked about my sickly looking
houseplants, and my skimpy tomato plants. I had,
of course, heard of Miracle-Gro products. What
gardener hasn't? But I had never tried it for myself.
When I finally did, the results were phenomenal. It
seemed that no matter what I was trying to grow, it
grew better after a few doses of this seemingly
magic potion. Intrigued by its success, I went to the
Miracle-Gro web page where I read that "Miracle-
Gro is a household name and by far the leading
brand in plant foods. More than 30 million people
use Miracle-Gro . . . to grow bigger, better plants,
flowers, and vegetables every year." They also
claim that Miracle-Gro is "ideal for all plants,
outdoors and indoors," "starts to work fast so you
see results fast," "is available almost everywhere,"

and, best of all, it is "guaranteed"! Those are some pretty impressive claims.

While I'm not trying to sell Miracle-Gro, I do know of another product that truly does fulfill all of those promises and more. The Bible is what I consider to be the best Miracle Grow product on the market. Like Miracle-Gro claims to be, the Bible truly is ideal for all people, starts to work fast so you see results fast, and is available worldwide in almost every language. It is guaranteed by the author himself who assures us that "All over the world this gospel is bearing fruit and growing, just as it has been doing among you since the day you heard it" (Col. 1:6). However, like any product, it only works if you use it. That's why God urges us to "desire the sincere milk of the word, that ye may grow thereby" (1 Pet. 2:2;KJV). Are you struggling in your walk with God, sickly in your spiritual growth, skimpy in your faith? Open up the Bible and try a good dose of His Miracle Grow!

Facing Up

Set your minds on things above, not on earthly things
(Col. 3:2).

I had hoped for more instructions or, for that matter, any instructions at all. My mail order package of 100 assorted fall bulbs had arrived with nothing but the bulbs themselves. This was my first attempt at planting bulbs. *No matter*, I thought as I stared at the various shapes and sizes. *I'll throw them all in the ground together and take my chances.* After the last bulb had been planted and I was cleaning up, I discovered the planting guide in the bottom of the bag. It said to "plant all bulbs with the tips facing up." It went on to explain why. "If their tips face down, they waste their energy trying to grow in the opposite direction." In other words, if the bulb was planted upside-down, it would have to curl around itself before it could even begin its climb to the surface. Even if it did manage to break through the ground it would have no strength left to produce a flower.

We can learn a lesson from those upside-down

plants. Like bulbs, we need to be pointed upward if we want to blossom to our fullest potential. When our focus is on God and on His blessings we will naturally maintain a positive attitude and a joyful spirit. We will easily rise above whatever difficulties we encounter along the way and ultimately reach even our highest goals in life. If we choose instead to allow our attention to be drawn downward, away from Him, and redirected toward our problems, we will quickly find ourselves stuck in the mud. Focusing on negative circumstances, or even on the world around us, drains our energy and steals our joy. Like bulbs pointed in the wrong direction, our spiritual growth will be stunted and our lives wasted. That spring only about half of my bulbs flowered, but those that did were a colorful reminder to keep looking up. Each of us can choose whether we will live in gloom or in bloom.

Go Organic

They tell how you turned to God from idols to serve the living and true God (1 Thess. 1:9).

One of the current gardening crazes is the organic garden. Environmentalists tell us it will save the planet. Health experts tell us it will save our bodies. About the only ones who don't like the idea of an organic garden are those who sell pesticides. The term "organic garden" can be applied to any kind of garden as long as only biological fertilizers and pesticides are used. Organic literally means "living" so the organic gardener uses living organisms rather than man-made or chemical products. Chemicals can cause health problems and aren't necessary for successful gardening if one knows what natural organisms to substitute. Organic gardening is accomplished through the use of such produces as animal manure, compost, grass, straw, and other natural residues. Biological pest control can be achieved through crop rotation and the use of pest-deterrent species of plants, as well as the release of sterile male insects and predators of pests. The key is in exclusively using what is all-natural or all-living as opposed to artificial or man-made.

The world is filled with people of all kinds of faiths, churches, and religions. However, many have substituted man-made beliefs and practices for what the Bible describes as a true faith in the living God. In Bible times, people exchanged faith in God for idol worship. These man-made objects had no power to save but instead, like using chemicals, had a most detrimental effect on those who worshiped them. Today, some have replaced idols with the worship of other man-made substitutes such as money, fame, and power. Others, instead of worshiping the living God, follow after other men such as self-proclaimed spiritual leaders, prophets, and gurus. It's never too late to get rid of the chemicals and start an organic garden. In the spiritual realm, the Bible assures us, "We are bringing you good news, telling you to turn from these worthless things to the living God, who made heaven and earth and sea and everything in them" (Acts 14:15). Why not go organic! That's really living.

God's household, which is the church of the living God, the pillar and foundation of the truth (1 Tim. 3:15).

A mulch is any material that is laid down on top of the soil around trees or plants. Gardeners use different kinds of mulches depending on what they most want to accomplish. There are two main kinds of mulches: summer and winter. Summer mulch remains in place year round. Its functions include reducing soil erosion, preventing weeds, conserving moisture, and regulating soil temperature. The materials used can be inorganic like plastic, newspapers, pebbles, or organic matter such as compost, pine bark, or buckwheat hulls. Inorganic mulches are often chosen for their attractive appearance such as in decorating the base of a tree. However, organic mulch has the additional benefit of adding organic matter and nutrients to the soil. Winter mulch is used to prevent soil from alternately freezing and thawing which can heave out plants leaving their roots exposed on the surface. It is applied after the soil freezes and should be removed in early spring. The best materials for winter mulch are those which are coarse textured such as straw, hay, or evergreen boughs.

We sometimes choose our mulch in the same way we choose a church. Our decision is based on what we most want to accomplish. Those who are primarily looking to fill a social need will often select a church based on outside appearance, opting for an attractive, albeit inorganic fellowship. Those who are spiritually hungry will seek out a church which provides organic matter or nourishment through strong biblically based teaching, and the obvious presence of the Holy Spirit in the lives of its members. Organic, by the way, means living! Those who seek a living church, a church filled with the Spirit of God, will also find a winter mulch, a group of fellow believers who will see them through the winter freezes. So choose your church carefully and remember, "He who has an ear, let him hear what the Spirit says to the churches. To him who overcomes, I will give the right to eat from the tree of life, which is in the paradise of God" (Rev. 2:7).

But it has now been revealed through the appearing of our Savior, Christ Jesus, who has destroyed death and has brought life and immortality to light through the gospel (2 Tim. 1:10).

It seems to happen almost overnight. I'll be enjoying the warm days of summer and wake up one morning to the nip of fall in the air and the trees ablaze with the colors of autumn. This dramatic and sometimes almost electrifying display is yet another tribute to the Creator's artistry. It is also a reminder of the inevitability of the end of summer, and the winter soon to follow. As the hours of sunlight become steadily shorter the sap in the trees slows and finally stops its supply to the leaves. All that glorious color is being produced as they die. The leaves finally fall to the earth, only to be replaced the following spring as the cycle starts again. Each season they appear in increased abundance as the growing tree matures. Then, come fall, they go out once again in another blaze of glory.

Each of us must face death one day. The Bible promises us that we, too, can go out in a blaze of glory. We are assured that "Death has been swallowed up in victory. Where, O death, is your victory? Where, O death, is your sting? The sting of death is sin, and the power of sin is the law. But thanks be to God! He gives us the victory through our Lord Jesus Christ" (1 Cor. 15:54–57). The dying leaves of autumn will be replaced by new life come spring. Thanks to Jesus, our lives can do the same. He willingly allowed himself to experience death knowing He would ultimately defeat it by His resurrection. We are told, "When you were dead in your sins . . . God made you alive with Christ. He forgave us all . . . that was against us and that stood opposed to us . . . triumphing over them by the cross" (Col. 2:13–15). Because He did, we can now have the assurance that our last breath on this earth will be followed by our first breath in paradise. Our Savior's death set ablaze a glory that will light our way into eternity.

Transformation

Formerly he was useless to you, but now he has become useful both to you and to me (Philem. 1:11).

My husband and I were out on our daily walk when we first noticed the small fenced-in area in our neighbor's yard about the size of a large sandbox. When we started seeing it being filled with dead plants, leaves, rotting tomatoes, and table scraps we realized it was a compost bin. Composting is the transformation of organic material (such as plant matter) into a soil-like material called compost. Living organisms such as insects and earthworms, and microorganisms such as bacteria and fungi all take part in the process of transforming waste material into compost. We forgot about the little compost bin until the following spring when we noticed that the fenced-in area had been transformed from a compost pile to a garden. All of the rotten food and dead leaves were now replaced by thriving new plants. Right there on top of the now nutri-ent-rich soil our neighbor planted a vegetable garden that eventually produced some of the most luscious tomatoes and squashes I've ever seen.

That transformation from garbage to garden demonstrated the natural recycling process God has built into His universe. God truly is in the transformation business, but His work goes far beyond the limits of nature. Our God transforms human lives as well. What others see as worthless, God sees as great potential. In His hands, lives that were once without hope are transformed into "a chosen people, a royal priesthood, a holy nation, a people belonging to God, that you may declare the praises of him who called you out of darkness into his wonderful light" (1 Pet. 2:9). This miraculous transformation is perhaps best described in the words of a familiar and beloved hymn: "Amazing grace, how sweet the sound that saved a wretch like me. I once was lost but now am found; was blind but now I see." If God can use rotten tomatoes to grow succulent new plants just think what He can do with a person who gives their life, just as it is, to Him.

Instead, they were longing for a better country — a heavenly one. Therefore God is not ashamed to be called their God, for he has prepared a city for them (Heb. 11:16).

The first clematis I ever saw was floating in a bowl of water, its gigantic pink flower literally filling the bowl. After learning that this extraordinary bloom came from a climbing vine, a few of those vines were quickly climbing in my own backyard. The planting instructions stated that the clematis needed to be planted with its "feet in the shade and its head in the sun." The clematis vine (a member of the *Ranunculaceae* family) will easily grow up to 12 feet. Most varieties produce single flowers ranging from one to ten inches in size. A few produce double flowers, or both single and double flowers. The blooms of the clematis often change color through the life of each flower particularly when grown in the sun. They need to be protected from the reflective heat of the sun, which is why it is so important to keep the "feet" of the plant in the shade.

We who are believers live on this earth along with the rest of mankind. In that sense, our feet are in the shade, or the darkness of this fallen world. For us to grow, then, we must keep our heads in the sun. We do this by refocusing from the world around us to the Savior who loves us. By putting our faith in Him we can be "sure of what we hope for and certain of what we do not see" (Heb. 11:1). The Bible's famous "faith chapter" lists several individuals who did just that. Some saw great miracles take place, but others, also equally credited for their strong faith, did not. No, "these people were still living by faith when they died. They did not receive the things promised; they only saw them and welcomed them from a distance. And they admitted that they were aliens and strangers on earth . . . they are looking for a country of their own" (Heb. 11:13–14). Having lived their lives with their heads in the sun they finally stepped from the shade into the eternal light of the Son.

Tools of the Trade

May the God of peace . . . equip you with everything good for doing his will, and may he work in us what is pleasing to him, through Jesus Christ, to whom be glory for ever and ever. Amen (Heb. 13:20–21).

Having the right equipment makes all the difference in the world. I found this out firsthand the day I tried to plant a tree without the proper tools. I was doing okay until my little shovel hit the first rock. After a long struggle and a broken shovel I finally gave up and went out to purchase some real gardening tools. I soon discovered there are more kinds of gardening gizmos than I'd ever dreamed of (most of which I bought on the spot). There are all kinds of shovels, spades, digging forks, and hand trowels for digging. There are wheelbarrows for transporting, watering cans, weeders, pruning sheers, gardeners' gloves, and cutting saws. One could also buy specialty items like bulb planters and trellises. For cleanup there were hoes and rakes. The next time I headed back out to try again I went armed with some serious equipment and what a difference it made! With the right tools the tree was planted in minutes.

My experience in planting a tree went from impossible to simple once I had the right tools. When God asks us to do something He sends us out fully equipped. He has already provided us with everything we need even before we ask. First, He has given us His Word. We are told, "All Scripture is God-breathed and is useful for teaching, rebuking, correcting and training in righteousness, so that the man of God may be thoroughly equipped for every good work" (2 Tim. 3:16–17). In addition, He has given each of us spiritual gifts perfectly suited for the unique role He has called us to. He has also given us each other. We are to use our gifts "to prepare God's people for works of service, so that the body of Christ may be built up" (Eph. 4:12). Above all, He has given us himself. With His Holy Spirit at work within us the impossible becomes simple or, as Jesus put it, "With God all things are possible" (Matt. 19:26).

The Experiment

Peacemakers who sow in peace raise a harvest of righteousness (James 3:18).

Their packet called them multicolored zinnias and they proved to be just that. From that one small package came brilliant orange flowers, fluorescent pinks, vivid yellows, and more. I particularly loved the pink ones. That's what led to my experiment. What would happen, I wondered, if I saved seeds exclusively from the pink zinnias? Would I get multicolored zinnias, or would they only grow pink flowers? The following year I got my answer. I saved seeds from several of the brightest pink flowers and planted them in a completely different area of the garden. When the new crops bloomed, there were nothing but pink zinnias. They came in numerous different shades of pink, but all were distinctly pink. I suppose that was completely logical. Could a pink zinnia seed really be expected to produce an orange flower? Or, as the Bible puts it, "Can a fig tree bear olives, or a grapevine bear figs?" (James 3:12). No, we are told,

"A man reaps what he sows" (Gal. 6:7). The Scriptures weren't speaking of zinnia seeds, however. Reaping what you sow is just as applicable to us.

We get out of life what we put into it. Those who live to please God will one day reap the rewards, while those who live only to please themselves will reap a far different harvest. We read that "the one who sows to please his sinful nature, from that nature will reap destruction; the one who sows to please the Spirit, from the Spirit will reap eternal life" (Gal. 6:8). When we give our lives to the Lord we are not only assured of His blessing, but are a blessing to others as well. Don't forget, however, that beautiful flowers don't grow overnight. Nor do beautiful, God-pleasing lives. Perhaps that is why He urges us to "not become weary in doing good, for at the proper time we will reap a harvest if we do not give up" (Gal. 6:9). Yes, we will reap what we sow someday, and I have the pink zinnias to prove it!

Sure Harvest

See how the farmer waits for the land to yield its valuable crop and how patient he is for the autumn and spring rains (James 5:7).

I saw a cartoon that pictured a man sitting on the ground in the middle of a garden. The ground had been tilled and the seeds just planted. Nothing had yet germinated. The man was wearing a bib, and was holding a knife and fork. An empty plate was on the ground in front of him along with a bottle of salad dressing. The caption read, "Eugene just doesn't have the patience for gardening." A lot of us gardeners can relate to Eugene when we first plant our crops, knowing it will be months of hard work if we are ever to have something to put on our supper plate. Most of us keep at it though, knowing that the feast awaiting us will be well worth our labors. For professional farmers there is much more at stake. They are dependent on their crops, not only to fill their own plates, but to provide for their needs for an entire year. It is no wonder, then, that the Bible uses the illustration of the farmer to define true faith saying, "Be patient, then, brothers, until the Lord's coming. See how the farmer waits for the land to yield its valuable crop and how patient he is for the autumn and spring rains" (James 5:7).

What the farmer is waiting for is a matter of great necessity for him and his family. But he goes about his business trusting that his labors will not be in vain. He plants knowing that crops will follow. He goes through the times of drought, weeds, tired muscles, and aching backs believing his efforts will ultimately pay off. Even setbacks and losses along the way will not stop him because he has set his eyes on the harvest that awaits him if he does not give up. We are told, "You too, be patient and stand firm, because the Lord's coming is near" (James 5:8). As sure as seeds produce plants and the land brings forth crops, our faith in God assures us of the feast He is preparing for us in heaven — and He's coming in person to take us there.

To God's elect, strangers in the world . . . who have been chosen according to the foreknowledge of God the Father, through the sanctifying work of the Spirit, for obedience to Jesus Christ (1 Pet. 1:1–2).

Go into any department store as the holiday season approaches and you'll probably find them. The Christmas amaryllis is a traditional gift plant that is artificially trained to bear its gigantic red blooms throughout the Christmas season. It is a welcome and festive addition in any home. What many don't realize is that the amaryllis, with a little extra help, can be transplanted outside to decorate the yard with its dazzling display of flowers. To accomplish this it is vital to transplant the plant as soon as possible. It was forced in the nursery to be the beautiful plant that sells in the store, but if it is to bloom outdoors it needs to adapt to the real world. Once planted, spent flowers should be removed and plenty of rich, quick-draining soil and fertilizer applied. One book I read suggested that the new amaryllis should be "treated as an honored guest in your garden." After all, this is not the environment it was raised in.

The day we give our hearts to the Lord is the day when we first come to full bloom in His spiritual nursery. But like the amaryllis plant, that should not be the end but the beginning of a whole new flower bearing life. God wants to transplant us back into the real world. However, as new believers, it is a world we are no longer a part of but are, instead, His honored guests here. Our true citizenship is in heaven with Him so we are now planted "as aliens and strangers in the world" so that others "may see your good deeds and glorify God on the day he visits us (1 Pet. 2:11–12). God tenderly oversees our growth and causes us to blossom. As those around us see the dazzling display of God's work in our lives they, too, can come to know the source of that beauty living within us. A day will come, however, when our season of bloom has passed. Then, like the amaryllis plant, we will be taken home for Christmas.

Cast all your anxiety on him because he cares for you (1 Pet. 5:7).

We've all had them. Those so-called "friends" who seem to do nothing but drain us. They are always taking and never giving, always needy and totally oblivious to any needs we might have. In the plant world this kind of relationship is known as parasitic. In parasitism one member of the relationship benefits while the other is harmed. Parasites generally absorb food from their hosts but may also receive water, minerals, and shelter. Plant diseases caused by parasites include wheat rust, corn leaf blight, corn smut, and Dutch elm disease. If a host dies from disease the parasite is also at risk of dying. As a result, some parasites and their hosts develop a form of mutual tolerance, but still not without some cost to the host.

The biggest difference between plant parasites and overly dependent human relationships is that as humans we can choose to do something about it. Rather than allowing ourselves to be dragged down by a relationship we have the option of ending the relationship or of setting some healthy boundaries. When necessary, we can also encourage the other person to seek professional help. As believers, we have an additional option. Along with the above options, we can also help the person learn to transfer their dependency to God. He is the only host who can turn a parasitic relationship into a mutualistic one. He actually desires for us to lean fully on Him, telling us to "Come to me, all you who are weary and burdened, and I will give you rest. Take my yoke upon you and learn from me, for I am gentle and humble in heart, and you will find rest for your souls. For my yoke is easy and my burden is light" (Matt. 11:28–30). When we point a friend to Jesus they will find Him sufficient to meet all their needs. When we share a mutual faith and dependency on the Lord with someone we often discover them to be a true friend after all.

Backcrossing

Through these he has given us his very great and precious promises, so that through them you may participate in the divine nature and escape the corruption in the world caused by evil desires (2 Pet. 1:4).

All of the magnificent garden flowers you see today are some form of hybrid. Hybridization is the crossbreeding of two species to create a plant with some characteristics of each parent. The goal is to capture the desirable traits of both parents in a single plant. Since undesirable traits are also passed along, it takes several generations of careful selection and rejection to create the desired product. Backcrossing is a variation of hybridization that is used to transfer into a desirable species a beneficial trait from an otherwise undesirable parent. At first, individual plants produced by backcrossing show a wide mixture of characteristics of both parents, but with continued backcrossing in approximately six or seven generations the variety again breeds true but now exhibits its new trait. Backcrossing is particularly useful for adding single characteristics to plants and has been used with great success to add such features as resistance to specific insects or diseases.

Each of us is the product of two different human parents and we exhibit traits of each, both good and bad. When we accept the Lord as our Heavenly Father, a process begins to take place in our lives that is similar to backcrossing. As we grow in our faith we begin to notice some of the bad traits we were born with begin to diminish. While we still have the characteristics of our physical parents, we see a new nature developing inside us that the Scriptures refer as the divine nature. The desirable traits of our human nature will remain, but some of the undesirable ones start to weaken, for "those who belong to Christ Jesus have crucified the sinful nature with its passions and desires" (Gal. 5:24). Our human nature is slowly being replaced by the nature of God through His Spirit living in our hearts. The more we let Him work in our lives, the faster His backcrossing process will be adding that single characteristic of His divine nature. In time, we'll not only look beautiful; we'll look like our Father.

A Super-Natural Enemy

The spirit of the antichrist . . . is coming and even now is already in the world. You, dear children, are from God and have overcome them, because the one who is in you is greater than the one who is in the world (1 John 4:3–4).

I honestly thought someone was trying to upgrade the local swamps, and even picked some of the lovely purple flowers to put in vases. Then I learned the truth about these attractive but dangerous weeds. Purple loosestrife (Lythrum salicaria) is a perennial herb with bright magenta flowers arranged in dense spikes on stems that grow up to six feet tall. It is an invasive noxious plant originally native to Europe, which is highly damaging to wetlands. It was introduced here as a garden flower, but has since escaped into the wild. Because it is not native to this area, it has no natural enemies. Wildlife does not use this plant but if anything, is deterred by it. Loosestrife is very prolific, producing over a million seeds per plant. Within a few seasons it can seriously impact a wetland area, replacing valuable native plants like bulrushes. This attractive-looking plant we willingly invited in has brought nothing but destruction to the local environment.

Sin is a lot like purple loosestrife. It is appealing to the eye and desirable, but once we invite it in, it quickly takes root. Then, the harder we try to remove it, the faster it seems to grow. We try to stop, time and time again, and fail. But then, sin was not native to this world. It was introduced here by Satan and, therefore, has no natural enemies. It does, however, have a supernatural one. Satan is powerful, but is certainly no match for his Creator. So when Jesus dwells within our hearts we have all we need to defeat this enemy. We read, "His divine power has given us everything we need for life and godliness. . . . he has given us his very great and precious promises, so that through them you may participate in the divine nature and escape the corruption in the world caused by evil desires" (2 Pet. 1:3–4). Environmentalists are still trying to find a solution to the purple loosestrife problem. We believers can claim our victory today.

To him who is able to keep you from falling and to present you before his glorious presence without fault and with great joy (Jude 1:24).

As a child, I loved to play in the fields behind our house. Often, while my mom was busy working in her beautiful gardens I would pretend that the endless assortment of wildflowers in the fields were my garden. I picked them by the armful and carefully prepared my own flower arrangements. When I came home for dinner I would bring one of my lovely bouquets for my mom. Ignoring the gorgeous cultivated flowers in her own yard she would always throw her arms around me and tell me what a beautiful bouquet I had made. Perhaps it is the warm feeling associated with those memories that still draws me into the fields to pick wildflowers. I love the challenge of creating beautiful floral arrangements from what some would consider mere weeds but I also remember the loving look on my mother's face as she accepted the bouquet I so proudly presented. For her, presentation was everything.

Presentation is the reason Jesus came to earth. Out of His great love for mankind, He came to pick armfuls of us to present to the Father. He places all who put their trust in Him in the bouquet He is preparing, and a lovely bouquet it will be. We read that "Christ loved the church and gave himself up for her to make her holy . . . and to present her to himself as a radiant church, without stain or wrinkle or any other blemish, but holy and blameless" (Eph. 5:25–27). His presentation, however, required the ultimate sacrifice. We are told, "But now he has reconciled you by Christ's physical body through death to present you holy in his sight, without blemish and free from accusation" (Col. 1:22). When I presented my dandelion bouquets to my mom, she didn't see weeds. She saw the expression of her daughter's love and those weeds became a glorious flower arrangement. When Jesus presents us to the Father He doesn't see sinners. He sees an expression of love from One who loved us enough to die for us.

The Arborvitae

He who has an ear, let him hear what the Spirit says to the churches. To him who overcomes, I will give the right to eat from the tree of life, which is in the paradise of God (Rev. 2:7).

When I decided to buy a tree for our summer home on the Saint Lawrence River I spent several months searching for the perfect tree. It had to meet several criteria including size (we wanted it to be huge), rate of growth (fast), and appearance (nothing short of the most beautiful tree in the world). Then one day I found that perfect tree I was looking for, perfect in ways I had not even imagined. I first discovered this tree in a garden catalog, which referred to it as "The Ultimate Fast-Growing Evergreen Screen." The tree was a giant arborvitae, which is Latin for "tree of life." When I heard this perfect tree was even biblical I began to wonder just how, out of all the trees in the world, this one earned its name. I learned that the arborvitae, or "tree of life" was given its name by Jacques Cartier (1491–1557), an early French explorer and mariner who was known for discovering the Saint

Lawrence River. It is believed that the lives of his crew were saved from scurvy by an Indian remedy made of tea brewed from the leaves of the arborvitae.

Jacques Cartier named this healing arborvitae after the tree of the same name found in the Bible. The biblical Tree of Life made its first appearance in the Garden of Eden but is not mentioned again until the very end of the Bible where it reappears at the throne of God. We read, "Then the angel showed me the river of the water of life. . . . On each side of the river stood the tree of life. . . . And the leaves of the tree are for the healing of the nations" (Rev. 22:1–2). If Jacques Cartier knew the Lord as his own personal Savior we will probably meet one day, at the foot of this amazing tree. The arborvitae was the perfect tree for our yard on the St. Lawrence River. It is also a reminder of all that awaits us at the throne of God.

On each side of the river stood the tree of life, bearing twelve crops of fruit, yielding its fruit every month. And the leaves of the tree are for the healing of the nations (Rev. 22:2).

In the beginning, God placed a man and a woman in a garden. The man and woman messed up and were forced to leave the paradise He had made for them. Though God removed mankind from the Garden, He did not remove the beauty and wonder of His creation from the rest of the world. He left us with a taste of what paradise was once like, so we would long for what it will one day be again. You see, in the end God will place us in another garden. All who have entrusted their lives to the Master Gardener will be welcomed into His garden paradise. It seems only fitting to end these garden gleanings with a glimpse of that glorious, heavenly garden that awaits us. This old, tired earth will be completely replaced by a new heaven and earth. Paradise will not just be restored. It will, in every way, be made brand new.

First, there will be a new lighting system. We

read, "The city does not need the sun or the moon to shine on it, for the glory of God gives it light, and the Lamb is its lamp" (Rev. 21:23). The new watering system will be the "river of the water of life, as clear as crystal, flowing from the throne of God and of the Lamb" (Rev. 22:1). There will also be a new kind of produce. We never got to taste the fruit of the tree of life in Eden. In the new garden, however, we will be granted a whole new access and "may have the right to the tree of life" (Rev. 22:14). Best of all, we will have a new kind of life in God's garden. We are told, " 'He will wipe every tear from their eyes. There will be no more death or mourning or crying or pain, for the old order of things has passed away.' He who was seated on the throne said, 'I am making everything new!' " (Rev. 21:4–5). Until then, I'll be waiting in my garden.

Journal Notes